SCHOLASTIC

Teaching With Favorite Back-to-School Books

BY IMMACULA A. RHODES

NEW YORK • TORONTO • LONDON • AUCKLAND • SYDNEY
MEXICO CITY • NEW DELHI • HONG KONG • BUENOS AIRES

Teaching Resources

Front cover and interior design by Kathy Massaro
Interior illustrations by Maxie Chambliss

ISBN: 0-439-52960-3

Published by Scholastic Inc.

Printed in the U.S.A.

1 2 3 4 5 6 7 8 9 10 40 11 10 09 08 07 06 05 04

Contents

About This Book

Welcome back to school! Whether you and your students are returning for another year at a familiar school or heading to a new one, *Teaching With Favorite Back-to-School Books* offers an array of activities designed to help you ease into the new year. Fresh, creative ideas related to books about going to school tap into the emotions, excitement, and energy stirred up by those special first days and weeks. Activities are designed to help children explore emotional and personal issues that arise with a new school year while also addressing cross-curricular areas to help you teach important language arts, math, science, social studies, and social skills right from the start.

Here is an overview of what you'll find in *Teaching With Favorite Back-to-School Books*:

- **Teaching Activities for Any Time:** This section includes ideas and reproducible activity pages that work well with assorted back-to-school picture books.
- **Lessons for Individual Books:** Beginning on page 9, you'll find lessons for seven favorite back-to-school books. Each lesson includes a summary, story discussion idea, a wide range of activities and projects designed to enrich students' learning across the curriculum, and one or more reproducible activity pages uniquely related to the title.
- **Activities for Teaching With Other Back-to-School Books:** Extend student learning with mini-lessons and reproducible activity pages for two additional back-to-school books.
- **Fabulous First-Week Festivities:** Conclude the first week of school with a fabulous celebration and the fun, memorable activities provided in this section.

Getting Started

- Decide how much time you plan to spend on your back-to-school unit. Be prepared to be flexible—you may find that spending additional time will help students work through difficult issues and better adjust to their new settings and schedules.
- Gather and read the books you plan to use for your back-to-school unit. Become familiar with the personalities, relationships, and conflicts of the characters in each book.

- Obtain multiple copies of as many titles as possible.
- Prepare a table display on which to feature your back-to-school books. Arrange other classroom areas to display book- and theme-related projects.
- If desired, have volunteers record each book on tape. Place the recordings in a listening center with copies of the corresponding books so that children can spend private time "reading" their favorites.

Connections to the Language Arts Standards

The activities in this book are designed to support you in meeting the following standards outlined by the Mid-continent Research for Education and Learning (McREL), an organization that collects and synthesizes national and state K–12 curriculum standards.

Uses the general skills and strategies of the reading process:

- Understands how print is organized and read
- Creates mental images from pictures and print
- Uses meaning clues to aid comprehension and make predictions about content

Uses reading skills and strategies to understand and interpret a variety of literary texts:

- Uses reading skills and strategies to understand a variety of familiar literary passages and texts, including fiction
- Knows main ideas or theme, setting, main characters, main events, sequence, and problems in stories
- Makes simple inferences regarding the order of events and possible outcomes
- Relates stories to personal experiences

Uses the general skills and strategies of the writing process:

- Uses writing and other methods to describe familiar persons, places, objects, or experiences
- Writes in a variety of forms or genres, including responses to literature

---

Source: *Content Knowledge: A Compendium of Standards and Benchmarks for K–12 Education* (3rd ed.). Mid-continent Research for Education and Learning, 2000.

Teaching Activities for Any Time

Enhance and extend students' learning experiences with this collection of ideas that work well with any back-to-school book.

First-Days Survival Kits

Invite children to pack survival kits for their choice of story characters. To begin, ask them to color and cut out the book bag pattern on page 8. Have them staple the left-hand side of a sheet of light-colored construction paper to the back of the cutout and trim it to match the book bag. To pack the bag, have students draw or glue on magazine cutouts of items that their selected story character needs or might use to ease into the first days of school. These items can include the usual school supplies—pencils, glue, scissors, and so on—as well as special transitional objects (such as stuffed animals), notes from parents, or pictures of loved ones. To extend, have children create and "pack" survival book bags for themselves.

First-Day Feelings

Excited, scared, or worried, each story character experiences some emotion about the first day of school. On chart paper, create a graph to show characters' feelings about this special day. First, label each column with a different emotion. Then list each character in the column that describes his or her first-day feelings. After determining the book characters' emotions, invite children to write their own names in the columns that describe their personal feelings about the start of school. Compare the results to learn which first-day emotion was the most common.

Postcard Perspectives

Use giant postcards to help children summarize character experiences and to invite others to read all about them. To create postcards, have children draw a picture of their favorite back-to-school book character (or story-related event) on tagboard. Ask them to include the title and author of the book with their drawings. Then have them turn over their postcards, draw a line down the middle, and write a message on the left side of the card. For their messages, have children write about a first-day school experience from the chosen character's perspective. Finally, help students address—and later, deliver—their postcards to children from another class.

Personalized Tales

Children will easily identify with the first-day feelings of most story characters. To personalize these stories, invite students to take the starring role in their favorite back-to-school books. Invite them to retell the stories using themselves as the main character and replacing the supporting characters with classmates, family members, teachers, and other familiar individuals. For a permanent record of their personalized tales, have children create illustrated books or tape recordings of their stories.

Schedule Shadows

When the story characters began school, they had to adjust to new schedules—just as your own students must do. To increase awareness of their schedules, invite children to pick a character to accompany them through their class routine for the day. Simply have them pretend that their chosen characters are shadowing them for the duration of the day. For example, when they have math, lunch, or recess, so do their characters. Display the class schedule in a prominent place. Then encourage children to follow it closely, preparing their "shadow" characters for upcoming transitions and activities. Ask children to keep a detailed journal of their imaginary experiences by recording each activity, its time, and the character's reaction or response to each activity throughout the day. Afterward, invite children to share and compare entries from their journal to find out how they imagined a storybook character would cope during a day in a true-life class.

Story Timelines

Have students create these fold-out story timelines to share with their families. First, have them color and cut out the book bag pattern (page 8). Ask them to write the title of a back-to-school book on the cutout. Then help them create a long strip of paper by gluing several half-sheets of 8 1/2- by 11-inch white paper together end to end, horizontally. Next, have children glue one end of the paper strip to the bottom of the book bag and then accordion-fold the strip to fit behind the bag. Ask them to draw the sequence of events from their selected story on the panels of the folded paper strip. To use, students unfold their timelines one panel at a time to retell the story to classmates or family members.

Book Bag Pattern

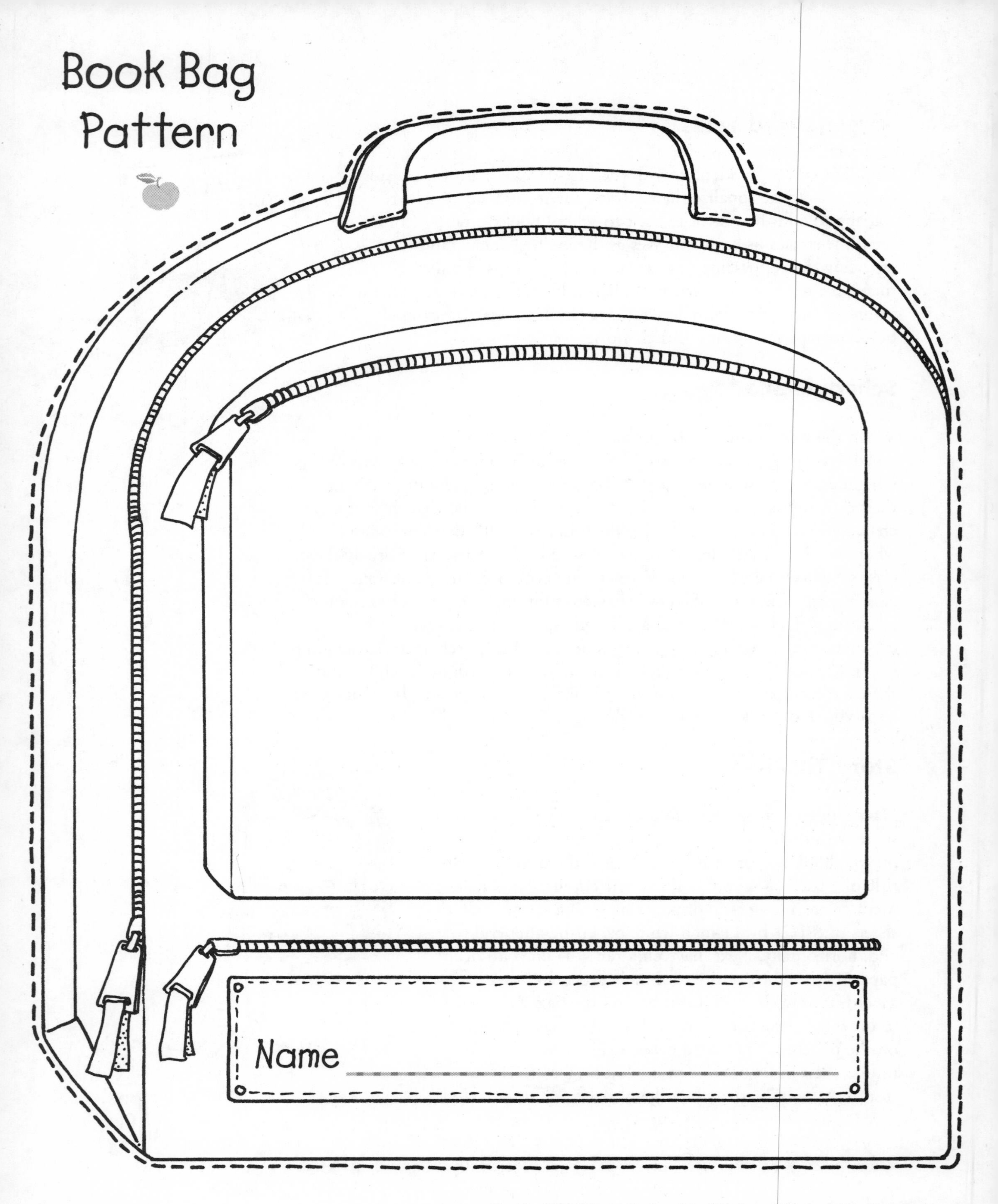

First Day, Hooray!

BY NANCY POYDAR
(HOLIDAY HOUSE, 1999)

It's almost fall and the town is hustling and bustling with preparations for the first day of school. Ivy Green shops for school supplies, while Ms. Bell sets up her classroom. Mr. Handy cleans the floors, Miss Wheeler studies her bus route, and Mr. Masters checks his principal notes. When the day is done, everyone goes home to sleep. But their dreams are riddled with first-day disasters: forgotten lunches, lost name tags, unfinished floors, missed bus stops, and pajama principal "suits." The sunrise chases all the anxious dreams away, though, and the first day gets off to a great start for everyone. Hooray!

Explain that many people contribute to preparing for the first day of school. Ask children to name some of them. What kinds of things do these people do to help get ready for the big day? Encourage children to think beyond the school walls and to include people in the community who also help in the preparations (such as police officers, doctors, and store owners). Invite children to share their personal and family experiences about preparing for the first day.

Extending the Book

Seasons of School (Science and Math)

School usually starts at the end of summer, when leaves are just beginning to change to fall colors in many regions of the country. What other seasons do children experience during a school year? To help them learn the seasons of school, display a calendar for each month of the year. Find the date that fall begins. Then invite a volunteer to dot each day of fall with a color marker. Have other volunteers use a different color marker to dot the days of winter, and then spring and summer. After color-coding the seasons, help children find the dates on which school begins and ends. Which seasons overlap

What's in a Name?

Write each character's name from the story. Ask children to tell how each name reflects that person's occupation. Challenge students to make up names to go with their classroom jobs, such as Mr./Ms. Broom for the class sweeper, Mr./Ms. Washer for the table-wiper, and so on.

First-Day Dreams

Some people have dreadful first-day dreams, and others have delightful ones. Ask children to draw their first-day dreams on large dream bubble cutouts. Then have them edge their cutouts with stretched pieces of cotton. Display the dream bubbles with the title "First-Day Dreams."

the school year? Invite students to describe weather conditions related to each season. Then, to extend, help children find holidays and special days and tell which seasons these occur in.

Workers and Worries (Social Studies and Language Arts)

Ms. Bell, Mr. Handy, Miss Wheeler, and many others all have important jobs to do to prepare for the first day of school. Ask children to name the jobs mentioned in the book and the workers who perform those jobs. Write each person's name on a chart and add his or her first-day worries. Then encourage children to name other school workers, such as cafeteria servers, the librarian, computer lab teacher, art teacher, music teacher, school secretary, and even volunteers. Add these people to the chart. Ask students to name a first-day worry that might concern each of these workers.

Worker	Worry
Miss Wheeler	learning her route missing a stop
Mr. Handy	not finishing his cleaning in time children walking on wet floors
Ms. Bell	getting her room ready having a name tag for everyone
Cafeteria Servers	having enough food spilling food
Mr. Masters	putting signs up in ti having the right paper

All for Fall, All for School!

(Language Arts and Science)

Throughout the book, outdoor illustrations are sprinkled with falling leaves. What season does this suggest to students? Explain that in fall, in some regions of the country, the leaves change color, break away from the trees, and float to the ground. Then invite children to make personalized leaves to use on a fall class display. First, have them color and cut out the leaf pattern on page 12. Then help them cut out the circle on their leaves and back it with a picture of themselves. Or, if a picture is not available, have them draw their face in the circle. Next, have them add a drawing of their body. Finally, ask children to write or dictate a sentence about how they are "falling for" (or like) school. Display the leaves on a large tree background with the title above.

Daily Routines (Language Arts, Social Studies, and Art)

Ivy and her classmates started a new school routine on their first day of school. Help reinforce children's school-related routines with puppets and role-playing. First, give students the bus and puppet patterns (page 13), a sheet of yellow construction paper, and a craft stick. Then have them follow the directions below to make the pieces. Invite students to use the puppets, individually or in pairs, to role-play their daily routines (they can incorporate the bus into their routines even if they don't ride a bus to school). Encourage them to set up additional props to represent home and school scenes for their role-playing.

1 Color and cut out the bus pattern. Cut out the window openings and cut along the door where indicated to create a flap.

2 Glue only the edges of the sides and top of the bus to the yellow construction paper, leaving the bottom edge free. Cut out the bus shape from the yellow paper.

3 Have students draw a picture of themselves on the puppet pattern. Then direct them to cut out the pattern and glue it to a craft stick handle.

4 To use, students open the bus door, "walk" their puppet onto the bus (between the two layers of paper), and position it in a window opening. Suggest that students invite a friend's puppet to join theirs on the bus. When the passengers have boarded, they can close the door and get rolling.

Froggy Goes to School by Jonathan London (Viking, 1996).

A dream makes Froggy just a bit nervous about his first day of school. But he soon learns that he has nothing to worry about. School's a big hit with this lovable critter—even if it is hard for him to sit still long enough to learn!

Look Out Kindergarten, Here I Come! by Nancy Carlson (Viking, 1999).

Henry is so ready for kindergarten! But when he reaches his classroom door, anxious thoughts overcome him and he begs to go home. With the help of his teacher, Henry's fears soon fade, and he's once again ready to join the fun that awaits him in kindergarten.

Vera's First Day of School by Vera Rosenberry (Henry Holt and Company, 1999).

Vera's first-day excitement freezes into fear, and she heads home to hide under her bed. Surprised to find her child at home, Mother reassures Vera and helps ease her fears. Then Vera returns to school to enjoy the rest of the day with her new teacher and friends.

All for Fall, All for School!

leaf pattern

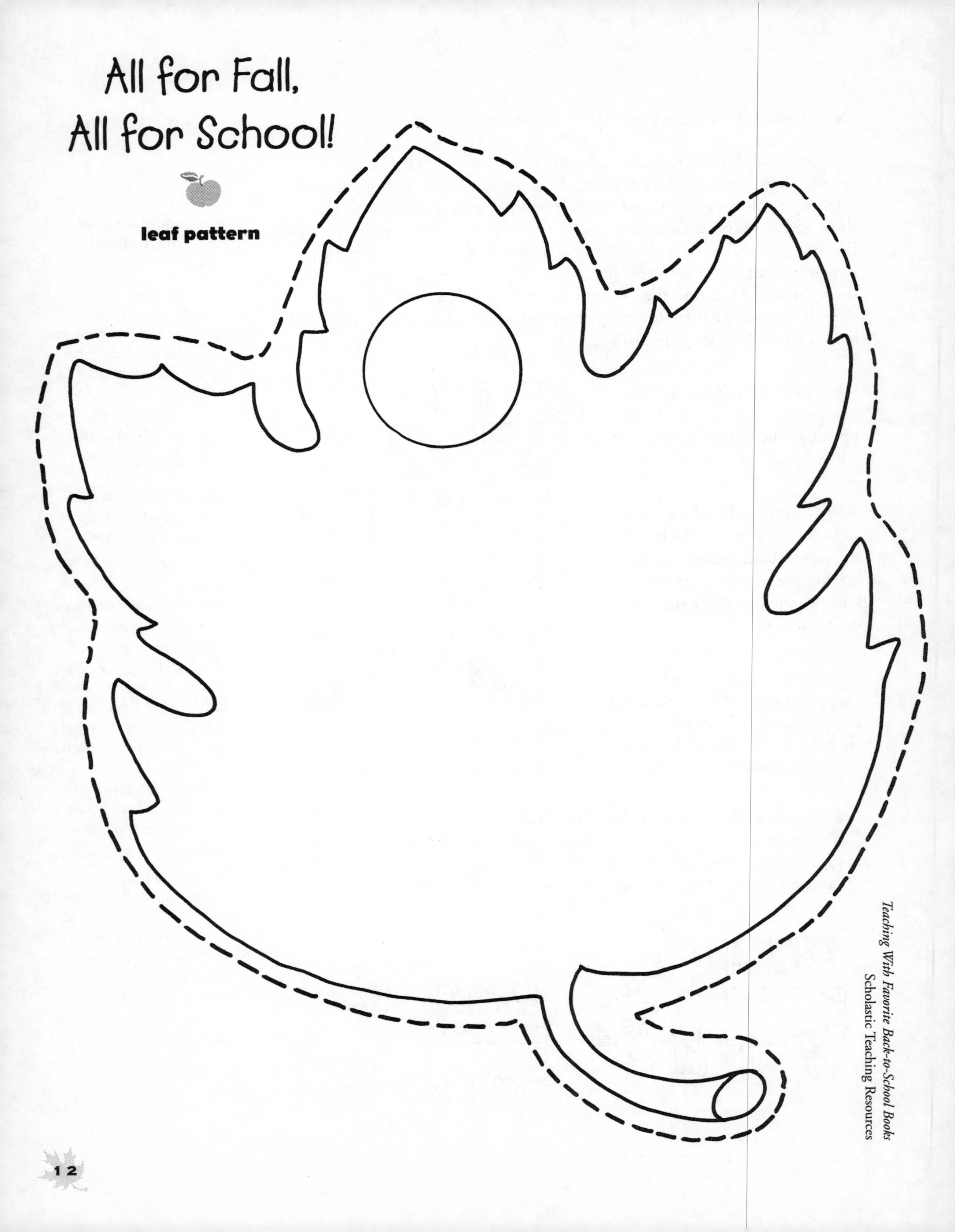

Daily Routines

bus and puppet patterns

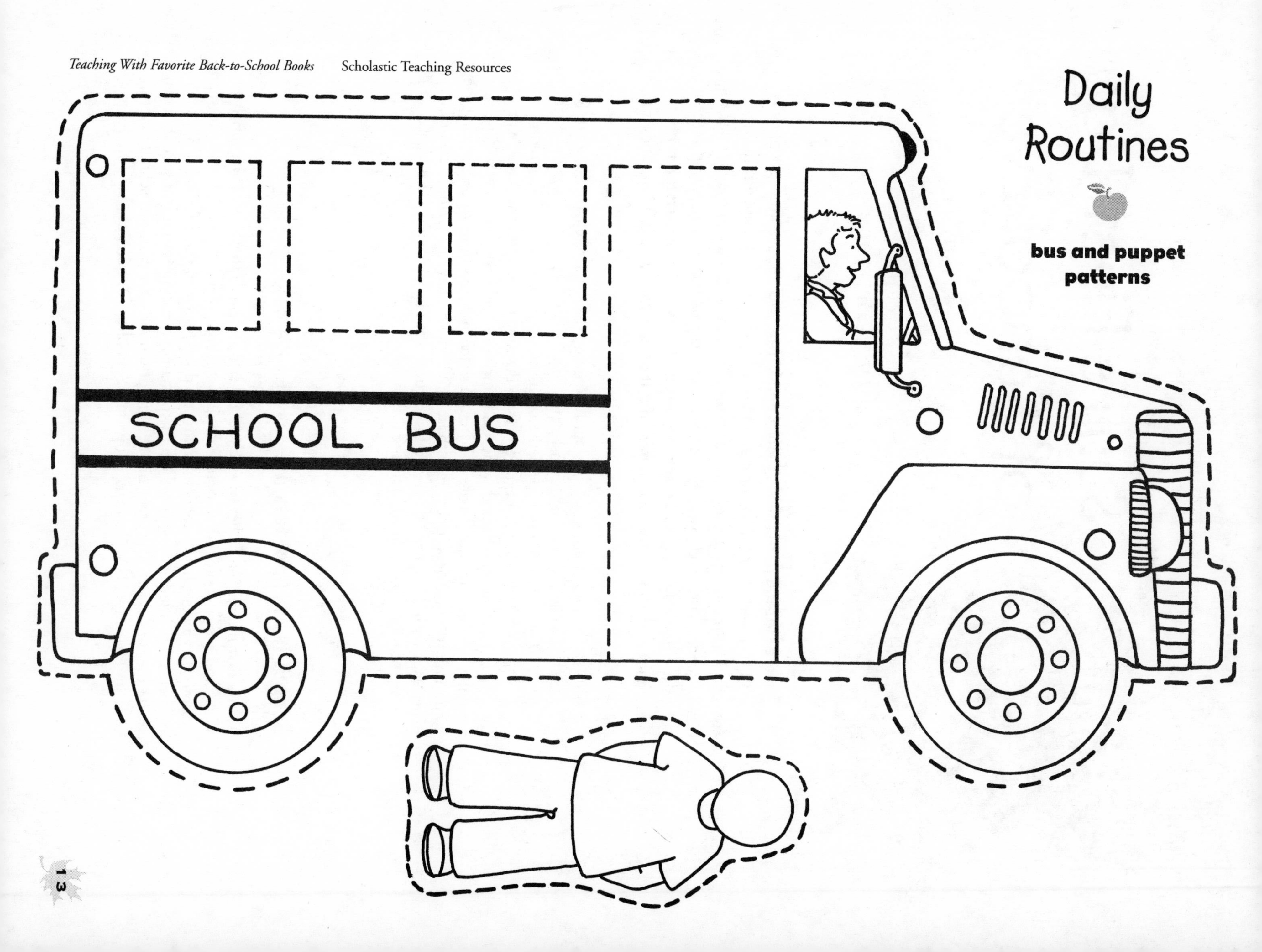

Sumi's First Day of School Ever

BY SOYUNG PAK
(VIKING, 2003)

Before starting at her new school, Sumi learns two things: what people say in English to ask for her name, and how to say her name in English. Equipped with this limited use of the English language, Sumi approaches her first day of school with much anxiety. To her, school seems lonely, scary, and mean. But as the first day progresses, she realizes that her teacher understands her fears, that classmates are nice to her, and that new friends are all around her.

Poll children to find out how many speak a language other than (or in addition to) English. How many have been in settings in which others did not speak the language they understand? Ask children who have had such experiences to describe the feelings that arose when they weren't able to understand what was being said. Did they find ways other than speaking to communicate? Invite children to share their solutions to overcoming the communication barriers. Encourage those children who have not had a personal experience with a language barrier to brainstorm ways in which they think successful communication can occur in such a situation.

Extending the Book

School Is . . . Booklets (Language Arts and Art)

Sumi's first impression of her new school led her to believe that school was lonely, scary, and mean. Do children ever feel this way about their school? Ask them to share reasons they might have experienced (or still do experience) these feelings. What happened (or might happen) to help them change their impressions of school? Then invite them to share their other impressions of school—for example, school as a fun, nice, and friendly place. To make individual School Is . . . booklets, have students stack a few sheets of 8 1/2- by 11-inch white paper onto a sheet of construction paper, fold the pages in half, and staple them together along the fold. Then ask them to write "School is . . ." on the front cover of their booklets and across the top of each inside page. Have children complete and illustrate the sentence frame on each page. Invite them to share their booklets with the class.

Hello Mural (Language Arts and Art)

Before going to school, Sumi learned the English response to "What is your name?" Create a large wall mural to help children get acquainted with one another by answering this same question. Invite a few children at a time to draw large self-portraits on a length of bulletin board paper. Encourage them to include in their drawings things that reflect their individuality and personality (for example, children might show themselves in a sports uniform, holding a pet, or doing a favorite activity). When finished, ask each child to draw a speech bubble and write "Hello, my name is ___________." Display the mural with the title "What Is Your Name?" Give each child a turn to tell the class about his or her self-portrait and unique qualities.

Memory Glasses (Language Arts)

To Sumi, her new school looked big, confusing, and scary. In addition, she didn't have a single familiar face with whom she could share eye contact or a welcoming smile. Experiencing the first day of school through Sumi's eyes helps to emphasize how people are affected both by what they see and how they perceive it. Invite children to make a simple pair of glasses by stapling together two toilet-paper tube rings and adding pipe-cleaner earpieces, as shown. Then ask them to quietly reflect on the time they first saw their school, new classroom, and new classmates. Did the school seem big? The classroom confusing? Classmates friendly? Did anyone make eye contact with and greet them? How did their view of these people and surroundings make them feel about school? Invite children, one at a time, to put on their memory glasses and share their experiences with the class.

Helpful Parents

Sumi's mother helped her prepare for the first day of school. Invite children to share ways in which their parents or caregivers helped them prepare for the big event. Then encourage them to make cards to express appreciation for their parents' or caregivers' support.

David's Drawings by Cathryn Falwell (Lee & Low Books, 2001).

David's simple drawing evolves into a colorful, detailed scene as one child after another adds to it. The result: a beautiful work of collaborative art and a classroom full of new friends for David.

Dear Whiskers by Ann Whitehead Nagda (Holiday House, 2000).

Jenny's letter-writing project to her second-grade pen pal is a disaster until she discovers the young girl doesn't speak English. Then Jenny's embarrassment turns to understanding—and a helpful solution.

Moses Goes to School by Isaac Millman (Frances Foster Books, 2000).

Although deaf, Moses and his classmates enjoy all the activities of a typical school day and more. How do they communicate? By signing words with their hands!

Say It With Expression (Language Arts, Social Studies, and Drama)

Although Sumi did not speak the same language as the boy, his expressions and gestures helped her understand the emotion and attitude conveyed by his words. Ask children to watch closely as you tell a story that incorporates a variety of character emotions and attitudes (perhaps a familiar fairy tale, such as Goldilocks and the Three Bears). Can they identify your emotions or attitudes by watching your facial expressions and hand gestures? Explain that these can be used to communicate kindness, rudeness, sadness, excitement, fear, and much more, even if a listener doesn't understand the spoken words. To let children experience this first hand, cut out multiple copies of the cards on page 17. Put the picture cards in one basket and the sentence cards in another. Invite a volunteer to draw a card from each basket. Then have the child read the sentence card, using expressions, gestures, and a tone of voice that convey the emotion or attitude shown on the picture card. Ask the class to describe what the child is trying to communicate.

Friendship Pledge (Language Arts and Character Development)

Both Sumi and her new classmates have a challenge ahead of them: she must learn to be a friend as the new kid, while they must learn to be a friend to the new kid. Recite this friendship pledge with children to help them understand some things it takes to grow a friendship from either perspective. Then discuss specific ways in which new and returning students in your school can show friendship to each other.

Friendship Pledge

I pledge (to/as) the new kid,
'til this school-year end,
To be an everyday pal,
a buddy, and a friend.

I pledge (to/as) the new kid,
'til this school-year end,
To smile, praise, and share,
and to lend a helping hand.

Collaborative Sand Drawings (Art and Character Development)

When Sumi and her classmate discovered a common interest in drawing in the dirt, they forged a bond of friendship—without speaking a word to each other! Set out a few shallow trays of sand and a pair of craft sticks with each tray. Randomly pair up students. (Put three in a group if you have an odd number of students.) Challenge students in each pair to create a collaborative sand drawing, without talking to each other. Afterward, have them describe their experiences. Were they able to understand each other without using words? How? Can similar methods be used to communicate with those who speak a different language?

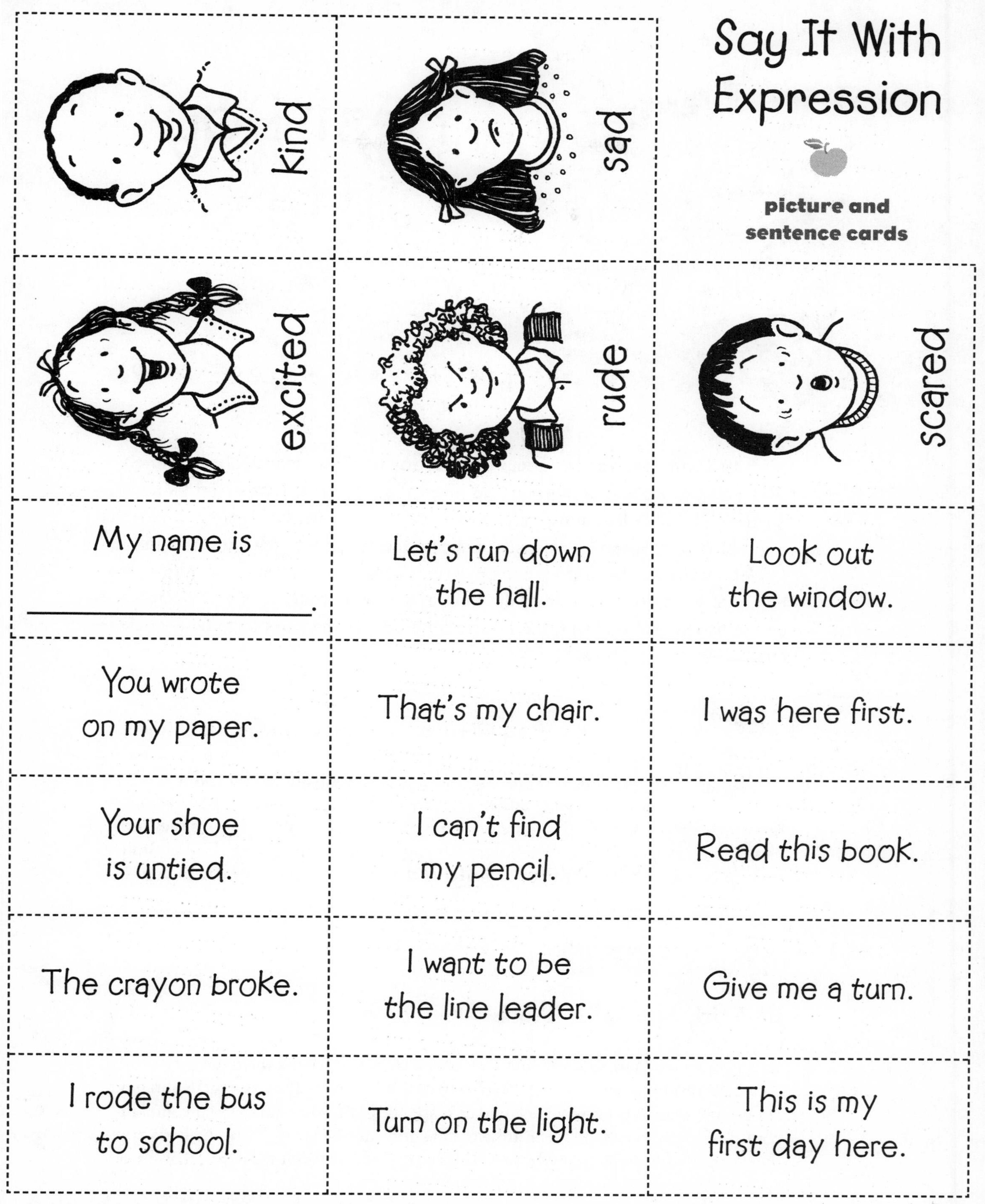

Say It With Expression
picture and sentence cards
kind
sad
excited
rude
scared
My name is ________.
Let's run down the hall.
Look out the window.
You wrote on my paper.
That's my chair.
I was here first.
Your shoe is untied.
I can't find my pencil.
Read this book.
The crayon broke.
I want to be the line leader.
Give me a turn.
I rode the bus to school.
Turn on the light.
This is my first day here.

First Day Jitters

BY JULIE DANNEBERG
(WHISPERING COYOTE, 2000)

Filled with reservations about her first day at a new school, Sarah tunnels down to the end of her bed and refuses to come out. That is, until Mr. Hartwell gives her five minutes to be dressed and downstairs. Feeling sick, weak, and breathless, Sarah summons up the courage to get into the car and head to school. On arrival, her enthusiastic principal whisks the nervous Sarah down the hall, into her classroom, and to the front of the room. Then, with all eyes focused on the two people up front, the principal introduces the class to its new teacher—Mrs. Sarah Jane Hartwell!

Ask children if they wanted to stay home on the first day of school. Divide the class into two groups according to their responses: "Yes" or "No." Then, beginning with the Yes group and ending with the No group, invite children to explain why they preferred either staying home or going to school. Continue by inviting volunteers to share reasons they are happy to be in school today. Then wrap up your discussion by giving children smiley stickers and telling them that you're glad that they came to spend the day in your class.

Extending the Book

He Said, She Said (Language Arts)

Point out to students that the first part of the story is told in a dialogue (or conversation) between Sarah and Mr. Hartwell. Then reread the story, encouraging children to think about which character is speaking. As you read, have the girls in your class raise their hands each time Sarah speaks in the story. Have the boys raise their hands when they hear Mr. Hartwell's part read. Afterward, explain that, in print, quotation marks are used to set off a speaker's exact words. Show how quotation marks are used in the book. Continue by telling students that speech bubbles are also used to show a person's spoken words. Ask them to think about a conversation they have had with someone (for example, a parent, sibling, or even pet) about the first day of school. Then have children draw themselves engaged in the conversation. Ask them to write and circle each speaker's words with a speech bubble. Invite children to share their dialogue cartoons with the class.

Who's There? (Science)

Show students the two-page spread on which the police and children are searching for Sarah. Draw their attention to the shadows on the floor. What's making the shadows? How? If Sarah were in the chair, what kind of shadow would they see? Explain that a shadow is created when something blocks the path of a light. A shadow takes the form of the object that causes it. Give children flashlights and let them experiment with creating shadows in the room. Then play this guessing game to help children become more familiar with one another. First, suspend a white sheet from the ceiling so that it touches the floor. Place an adjustable desk lamp and a chair behind the sheet, with the chair positioned sideways between the lamp and sheet. Next, divide the class into groups of three or four. Have one group at a time sit on the floor behind the sheet. Then ask the children to take turns sitting in the chair to cast their shadows onto the sheet (you may need to adjust the distance and angle of the lamp to get a well-defined shadow image of the child). Ask the class to name the mystery child in the chair. Did they guess correctly? What clues helped them guess? Continue until each student has had a turn to be the mystery child.

Diagnosis: Jitters

Jitters is another word for nervous, anxious, or excited feelings. What did Sarah say, feel, or do that indicated that she had a case of the jitters? Have children ever had similar symptoms? Invite them to tell what prompted the jitters and to describe how the jitters made them feel and act.

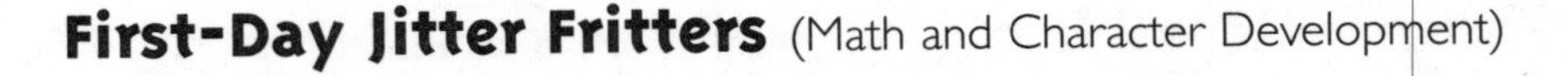

Jitter Critter

As Sarah worked through the first-day jitters, her cat was there to sympathize with and comfort her. Do any students have a jitter critter—a pet, stuffed animal, or doll that comforts and helps ease their fears and anxieties? Invite children to tell about their jitter critters. Later, send them to the art center to draw, paint, or craft models of their special comfort critters to share with the class.

First-Day Jitter Fritters (Math and Character Development)

Measure, mix, and munch away those first day jitters with some tasty jitter fritters. Before making these single-serving snacks, tell students that, like Sarah, most people experience mixed feelings on the first day of doing something new. Explain that each ingredient in this recipe represents a possible first-day feeling or experience. As children stir up their treats, share what each ingredient represents (as shown on the recipe, or make up ideas of your own):

First-Day Jitter Fritters

(makes one serving)

1/4 cup raisin bran *(for the nervous jiggles and lumps children feel inside)*

3 teaspoons peanut butter *(for new friends to stick with)*

1 teaspoon powdered sugar *(for fun things sprinkled throughout the classroom)*

1 teaspoon light corn syrup *(for the teacher's reassuring smile)*

3 teaspoons powdered milk *(for new ways to learn and grow)*

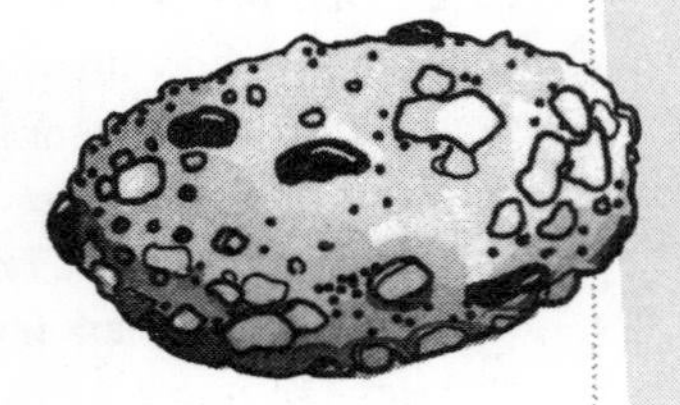

Mix all the ingredients in a bowl. Shape the mixture into a patty, drop it into a bag of powdered sugar, and then gently shake the bag to coat the patty with sugar. Remove the "fritter" and enjoy!

(NOTE: Check for food allergies before serving.)

Calm and Chaos (Language Arts)

After imagining a chaotic first-day classroom scene, it's no wonder Sarah preferred staying in bed! Turn to the two-page spread (near the front of the book) showing a pleasant, well-behaved class on the left and the same class "in action" on the right. Write a made-up name for each pictured child on sticky tabs (avoid using names of students in your class). Stick each tab to the corresponding child on the left page. Prop the book on a book stand in the writing center. Then invite visitors to the center to pick a child from the picture. Ask them to write a short, imaginary account of their chosen child's first day of school from that child's perspective. Encourage them to include a description of what prompted the child to behave as he or she did on the right page of the spread. During group time, display the two-page spread and invite children to share their stories with the class. To extend, children can make puppets to represent their chosen story students and then use them to act out skits about class activities and events.

Teacher-in-a-Lunchbox (Language Arts and Social Studies)

Most likely, Mrs. Sarah Jane Hartwell carried food in her lunchbox. But, to help children get to know you better, you can carry a bit of yourself in your school lunchbox. First, fill a lunchbox with photos and small items that represent you. Include pictures and things that will prompt children to guess information about you and your interests (for example, a crayon of your favorite color, a small stuffed animal to represent your pet, the cover jacket to your favorite CD, a picture of a sport you enjoy, a charm representing a special place or activity, and so on). If possible, include enough things to equal the number of children in your class. Then pass your lunchbox to children and invite them to remove an article from it. Encourage them to ask you questions about the article and then try to guess how it is significant to you. As children get to know all about you, use their interest as a springboard to get to know them better, too.

A First-Day Toast (Language Arts)

This story gives students a new and different way of looking at you—their teacher. Perhaps children are now curious about whether or not you had (or have) the first-day jitters. Share the feelings you experienced up to and on the first day of school. Also, talk about feelings you expect to have in the upcoming weeks—relief, satisfaction, comfort, and so on—as you and the children become more familiar with each other and class routines and activities. Discuss your feelings positively and with honesty. This will help children understand that adults get the jitters over some of the same things they do and that it may take time to work out these feelings. After discussing, remind children that Mr. Hartwell gave Sarah toast for breakfast. She deserved the treat for her efforts, but she also deserved another kind of toast—praise and a pat on the back—for making it through the first day of school! Copy and fill out the certificate (page 22) for each child in your class. Pass the certificates out to "toast" children for their first-day efforts. Then invite each child to reciprocate by filling out a certificate for you. (Note: The certificates can serve as a first-of-year writing sample for your records.)

Book Links

I Don't Want to Go Back to School by Marisabina Russo (Greenwillow, 1994).

Older sister Hannah teases Ben about his "what if" anxieties over the new school year. But the first day brings relief to Ben's worries—and a comical twist to Hannah's experience!

Miss Nelson Is Missing by James Marshall (Houghton Mifflin Company, 1977).

Dreading her unruly class every day, Miss Nelson decides that something must be done. Many days and one strict substitute teacher later, Miss Nelson returns from a "leave of absence" to find a kinder, more considerate class.

Tibili: The Little Boy Who Didn't Want to Go to School by Marie Leonard (Kane/Miller Book Publishers, 2002).

Tibili is convinced that school is a waste of time. But when he finds the Box of Knowledge and discovers that he can't read the directions for how to open it, Tibili has a change of heart and rushes home to ask his mom when school will start.

Toast Certificate

Congratulations,

(name)

A toast to you for coming
on the first day of school!

I'm glad you came to school because

Presented by

(name)

Will I Have a Friend?

BY MIRIAM COHEN
(MACMILLAN, 1967)

Pa reassures the anxious Jim that he will have a friend at school. As Jim goes through the day, however, he wonders where that friend is. To him, it seems that everyone has a friend to work, laugh, and play with. Everyone, that is, except him. Then, at rest time, Jim discovers that Paul and he have a common interest. As a friendship develops, the two new classmates enjoy the rest of the day together. After school, Jim happily tells Pa the good news—he has a friend at school!

Ask children to think about when they first met their closest friends. Did they become friends instantly? What happened to help them know that they wanted to be friends with that particular person? How long did it take for a friendship to grow? Explain that, often, friendships take time to develop. Invite children to share their views on why building a friendship might take time. Then discuss ways in which friendships often develop—from sharing common interests and activities to having similar backgrounds or experiences to spending time together and getting to know each other. Invite students to tell about the ways some of their own friendships developed and grew.

Extending the Book

Good-Friend Vests (Language Arts and Social Studies)

Readers can identify Jim by his vest. Invite children to create vests to show off the good-friend qualities that they possess. First, help each child cut out a neck opening and armholes from a large, plain paper bag, as shown. Have them write their name in large letters on the back of the vest. Then ask them to add words or phrases that describe their good-friend qualities, such

Moon Cookies

For fun, Jim and his classmates bit their cookies into moon shapes. Let your class try this, too. Give children individual portions of refrigerated sugar-cookie dough to shape into circles. Bake the cookies according to package directions. During snack time, ask children to imagine their cookies are full moons. Instruct them to bite their cookies into half-moon, and then crescent-moon shapes. Explain that the moon resembles each of these shapes as it goes through its full-moon, half-moon, and quarter-moon (crescent shape) phases. (Check for food allergies before serving cookies to children.)

as "helper," "a great listener," and "shares favorite toys." Children can also draw pictures that show themselves displaying good-friend qualities. For instance, they might include a drawing of themselves building a block structure or reading a book with a friend. During Show-and-Tell time, invite children to put on their vests and take a turn telling about ways they are good friends to others. Later, you might ask children who are working or playing together to exchange vests so that they can see their own vest as reminders of their own good-friend qualities.

Shared Secrets (Listening Skills and Social Interaction)

In the story, friends Sara and Margaret share a secret. Prompt children to interact with their classmates in this fun, informative, secret-sharing game. To begin, pair up children and assign each pair a number. Then take aside pair 1 and whisper to the partners a school- or class-related secret, such as the custodian's name, the number for the music room, or the title of your storytime book. Have each of these children take aside one of the partners from pair 2 and whisper the same secret to him or her. In turn, pair 2 will whisper the secret to pair 3, pair 3 to pair 4, and so on, until it has been circulated to every student pair. To end the game, have each partner in the last pair tell his or her version of the secret. Then ask pair 1 to tell the original secret. Were the two final secrets identical? If not, how did they differ? How do the final secrets compare to the original one? After discussing, pair up students with different partners, reassign numbers to the pairs, and play again.

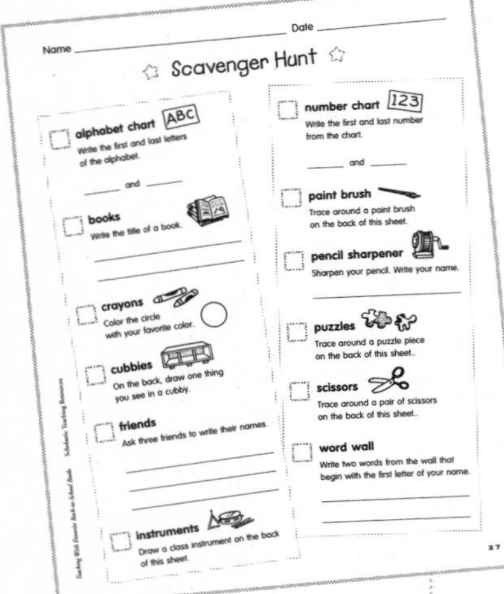

Name ______________________ Date ______________

Scavenger Hunt

- alphabet chart — Write the first and last letters of the alphabet. ______ and ______
- books — Write the title of a book.
- crayons — Color the circle with your favorite color.
- cubbies — On the back, draw one thing you see in a cubby.
- friends — Ask three friends to write their names.
- instruments — Draw a class instrument on the back of this sheet.
- number chart — Write the first and last number from the chart. ______ and ______
- paint brush — Trace around a paint brush on the back of this sheet.
- pencil sharpener — Sharpen your pencil. Write your name.
- puzzles — Trace around a puzzle piece on the back of this sheet..
- scissors — Trace around a pair of scissors on the back of this sheet..
- word wall — Write two words from the wall that begin with the first letter of your name.

Teaching With Favorite Back-to-School Books Scholastic Teaching Resources

27

Class Scavenger Hunt (Social Studies)

Scan the pages of the book with children to examine Jim's classroom. Do they see sights and scenes similar to their own classroom? To help students become more familiar with their classroom, conduct a simple scavenger hunt. To begin, give children copies of page 27. Review the directions for each item on the page. Tell students that any item used for the activity (such as scissors or puzzles) must be returned to its original place. Then send students on an exploration of the classroom to complete their scavenger hunt sheets. (If desired, you can set a 10- to 15-minute time limit on the activity.)

Mystery Interest Graphs (Math and Social Studies)

By just looking at Jim's classmates, it's impossible to tell which children have common interests or preferences. Students will find this true about their own classmates, too. During the first days of school, have children create interest graphs to help them learn which things they have in common with classmates. First, on chart paper, prepare a three- or four-column chart. Each day, choose a category, such as colors, ice-cream flavors, or sports. Write a different word belonging to the category on separate note cards (for example, *red*, *blue*, *green*, and *yellow* for colors). Attach each note card to a column heading. Then have children place a sticky note on their desk so that the sticky side is at the bottom and facing up. Ask them to write their name on the note. Then ask them to secretly stick their notes on the chart, name side down, to indicate their interests or preferences. Later, gather students around the chart. Invite children one at a time to pick a sticky note and then fold it up without removing to reveal the mystery child's name on the back. When all the names have been revealed, discuss with children the things they and their classmates have in common. Then compare the number of names in each column to discover which interest or preference is the most common in the class.

Where the Friends Are (Language Arts and Art)

In the story, Jim wondered where his friend was. Children will enjoy finding their class friends with this activity. First, have students draw self-portraits on quarter-size sheets cut from 8 1/2- by 11-inch white paper. Then enlist their help to create a large classroom scene on a length of bulletin board paper. When completed, cut enough 4-inch by 5-inch flaps in the scene to equal the number of students in your class. Behind each flap, attach a child's self-portrait. Then display the scene. To use, write each child's name on a slip of paper and put it in a basket. Invite a child to draw a name from the basket and recite "Where is my friend, ________?," filling in the name of the child on the slip of paper. Then ask the child to look behind the flaps of the classroom scene to find the named child. When the hidden child's self-portrait is found, invite that child to be next to draw a name from the basket.

Personal Pal Prints

Invite children to use people-shaped cookie cutters and paint to stamp people prints on large sheets of paper, being careful not to overlap the prints. After the paint dries, students can ask a different classmate to decorate each print to resemble himself or herself and then sign his or her name to the print. Have children title their pages "My School Pals."

Amanda Pig, Schoolgirl by Jean Van Leeuwen (Dial Books, 1997).

Happy to greet the first day of school, Amanda Pig discovers that not everyone shares her excitement. But her persistent positive attitude wins Amanda a new best friend by the end of the day.

Curious George Goes to School by Margret Rey (Houghton Mifflin, 1989).

During open house, George sets out to create a painting, but creates a big mess instead. In spite of his mischief, the clever monkey manages to save the occasion for everyone.

Sparky and Eddie: The First Day of School by Tony Johnston (Scholastic, 1997).

Assigned to different classes, best friends Sparky and Eddie decide not to go to school. But the buddies change their minds and soon discover that they can still be best friends.

Monkey See, Monkey Do (Art and Creative Movement)

In a moment of silliness, Jim's classmate Danny did a monkey imitation. In the same spirit of fun, and to promote class community, invite students to make these paper-plate monkey masks. Encourage them to wear the masks to play follow-the-leader or to perform simple tasks, such as sorting and shelving blocks.

1. Paint one 9-inch and two 6-inch paper plates with brown watercolor paint. Set the plates aside to dry.

2. Cut two eyeholes out of the 9-inch paper plate.

3. Glue one 6-inch paper plate to the large paper plate, as shown. Glue on two pompom nostrils and a yarn mouth.

4. Cut the other 6-inch paper plate in half. Trim each piece to resemble an ear. Glue an ear to each side of the monkey mask.

5. Punch a hole on each side of the mask. Tie a length of yarn to each hole.

Name ______________________ Date ______________

☆ Scavenger Hunt ☆

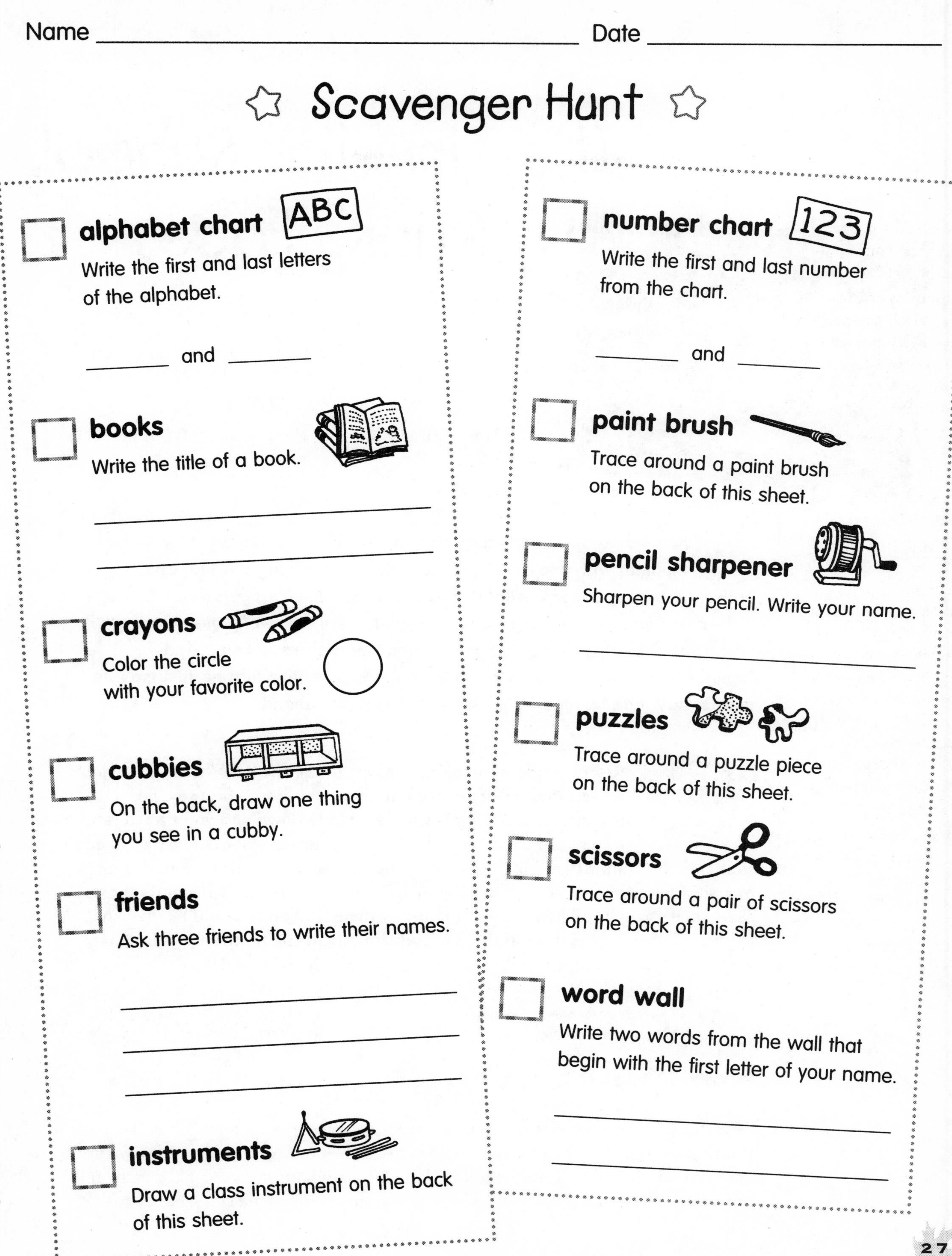

☐ **alphabet chart**

Write the first and last letters of the alphabet.

_______ and _______

☐ **books**

Write the title of a book.

____

____

☐ **crayons**

Color the circle with your favorite color.

☐ **cubbies**

On the back, draw one thing you see in a cubby.

☐ **friends**

Ask three friends to write their names.

____

____

____

☐ **instruments**

Draw a class instrument on the back of this sheet.

☐ **number chart**

Write the first and last number from the chart.

_______ and _______

☐ **paint brush**

Trace around a paint brush on the back of this sheet.

☐ **pencil sharpener**

Sharpen your pencil. Write your name.

____

☐ **puzzles**

Trace around a puzzle piece on the back of this sheet.

☐ **scissors**

Trace around a pair of scissors on the back of this sheet.

☐ **word wall**

Write two words from the wall that begin with the first letter of your name.

____

____

It's Time for School, Stinky Face

BY LISA MCCOURT
(BRIDGEWATER BOOKS, 2000)

When Mama announces that it's time for school, Stinky Face stalls the moment with one question after another involving unusual and unlikely school situations. *What if the kid-stuffed school bus gets a flat tire? What if the principal turns me into a werewolf? What if the teacher laughs herself silly? What if a spaceship lands on the playground?* Mama's reassuring, and sometimes equally silly, answers help Stinky Face realize that he just may be more ready than he thought for the fun school day ahead.

Rev up students' imaginations by asking them "What if" questions related to the story—without giving the story line away. For instance, ask, "What if your bus broke down and you had to ride to school with a clown?" "What if your classroom door was glued shut and you couldn't get in?" "What if aliens landed on the playground during recess?" Invite children to play out the imaginary situations in their minds and to share their thoughts. Then ask them if any of these situations would be likely to happen. Conclude the discussion by introducing them to Stinky Face, a little boy who has all these wild imaginings about school, plus a few more!

Extending the Book

Super Schedules (Math and Social Studies)

How did Mama know that it was time for Stinky Face to go school? Pose this question to students. When they provide "clock" as an answer, explain how we use clocks to set up and follow schedules. Then show students your daily class schedule and a large classroom display clock. Invite volunteers to set the clock hands to show the time for each activity on the schedule. (To help children learn their daily school schedule, do this activity each day during the first weeks of school.) Conversely, you can set the clock hands to a time for one of your daily activities. Then have children refer to the schedule to determine which activity starts at the time shown. To extend the activity and to help children understand the relationship between time and their home schedules, give them a copy of the reproducible on page 32. Direct them to cut out the clock hands and attach them to the clockface with a paper fastener. Then have them take the sheets home to complete with the help of their families. When they return their sheets the next day, invite children to share their home schedules with the class.

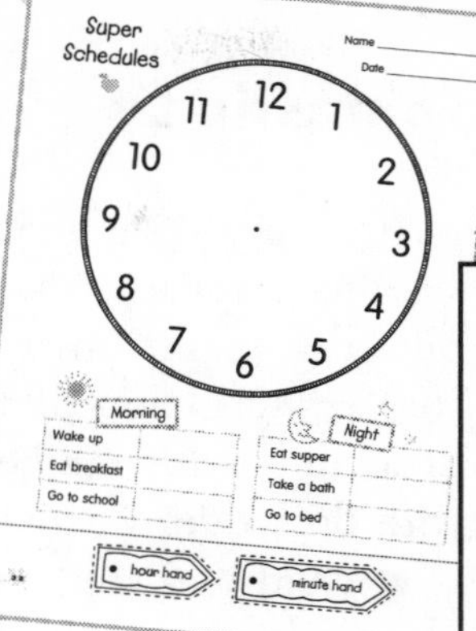
Super Schedules

Name ____
Date ____

Morning: Wake up / Eat breakfast / Go to school

Night: Eat supper / Take a bath / Go to bed

hour hand — minute hand

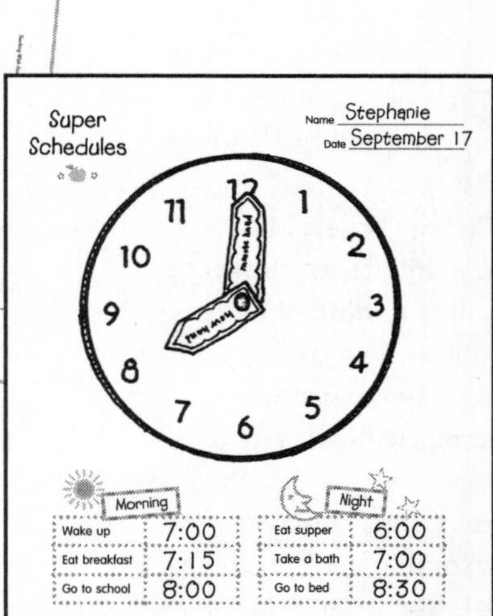
Super Schedules

Name Stephanie
Date September 17

Morning		Night	
Wake up	7:00	Eat supper	6:00
Eat breakfast	7:15	Take a bath	7:00
Go to school	8:00	Go to bed	8:30

Work Out the Worries (Language Arts)

Point out that the dialogue between Stinky Face and Mama followed an "If. . . then" pattern: for every worry expressed by the boy, Mama gave a response that provided a solution. Create this display to let children express their school-related worries and to work out possible solutions to them. Title a sheet of chart paper "If. . ." Then list children's school-related worries, such as "I missed the bus," "I got lost in school," or "I forgot my lunch." Read each situation aloud, adding "then" to the end of the sentence. Invite children to continue the sentence with possible ways to resolve the worry or dilemma. Then, for the display, write each situation on a separate sheet of paper. Post each page with an "If. . ." sign attached to the upper left corner and a "Then. . ." sign attached to the right of the page. Have students pick a situation from the display, write and illustrate their solution to it on a sheet of paper, and add their pages to the right of the corresponding situation. Invite children to point out and share their solutions with the class. Encourage them to add to the display in the future as they work out additional solutions to the posted situations.

Oodles of Obstacles

Stinky Face imagined lots and lots of obstacles to having a good day at school. List each of his imaginary obstacles on chart paper. Beside each, write Mama's response or solution to the obstacle. Discuss whether or not each obstacle and solution could really occur, highlighting the ones that could actually arise. Finally, ask children to explain what Mama meant in her last response to Stinky Face.

Get Moving

The story mentions two favorite children's songs: "Skip to My Lou" and "Hokey Pokey." Invite children to get moving to either or both of these tunes—with a creative twist. Simply replace parts of the songs with story-related words or phrases, then sing and dance away. For example, for the opening phrase of "Skip to My Lou," sing "Riding in a clown car," "Bouncing on a pogo stick," or "Climbing with the aliens." Or invite children to pretend they are fish or aliens doing the Hokey Pokey by adapting the words to fit the character (for instance, replace *hand* in "Put your right hand in" with *fin* or *tentacle*).

Fantastic 47 (Math)

In this story, 47 is very significant for its spell-breaking powers! Invite students to explore and break down the number 47 with this yummy activity. Give children a cup, a sheet of waxed paper, and a handful of *O*-shaped cereal loops. Ask them to count out 47 loops into the cup. Then have them group the loops by twos onto the waxed paper. How many groups of twos are in 47? Have children count the loops in increments of two. Next have students group the loops by threes, then fives and tens. How many of each grouping are found in 47? (You may wish to record this information on a chart.) Can they count the groups by the designated increments? Were children able to group the loops into exact sets for each number, with no loops left over? When finished, have children group the loops again, first by twos, then by threes, fives, and tens. After each, invite them to eat any leftover loops before continuing on to the next increment (the leftover loops will be 1, 1, 0, and 5, respectively). Ask them to subtract any pieces they've eaten from the total to figure the new number of loops they will group each time. Afterward, children can eat the remaining pieces to add up to 47 fantastic, spell-breaking cereal loops in their tummies! (Check for food allergies before serving cereal to children.)

A Class Imaginarium (Language Arts)

Nothing escaped Stinky Face's imagination—not even the fish! Cover a wide, lidless shoebox with blue paper. Decorate the sides of the box with an aquarium scene. Then talk with students about all the silly imaginings in the story. Ask them to share any far-out imaginings they may have had about the first days or weeks of school. Then, invite children to let their imaginations run wild as they write an imaginary school situation on a sheet of paper. On the other side, instruct them to draw a fish character (or any other underwater creature of their choice) involved in the imaginary situation. Have them deposit their drawings into the shoe box imaginarium. Later, pull out one fish at a time from the imaginarium and ask the creature's owner to show and tell the class about his or her imaginary situation.

Clowning Around With Verbs (Language Arts)

Enlist students' help in making a list of the many actions mentioned or shown in the story. A few include *drive, spin, bounce, fall,* and *dance.* Invite students to add other school-related actions to the list. After creating the list, explain that action words are verbs. To emphasize this special part of speech, cut 12-inch paper circles in half. Give one to each child to decorate and then shape and glue into a cone-shaped clown hat. After the glue dries, have them trim the edge of the cone into a zigzag or wavy design. Then ask students to wrap a 6-inch length of pipe cleaner around a pencil, slide it off, and poke it into the top of their clown hats. Help them secure the pipe cleaner on the inside of the hat with tape. Finally, invite children to don their clown hats and act out each verb on the list as you point to it.

Alien Goop (Math and Science)

Give children an out-of-this-world experience with these individual portions of alien goop. First, prepare a large copy of the alien goop recipe on posterboard, omitting the recipe name. Display the recipe with all the ingredients. Then explain that students will create a special substance. Ask them to examine the recipe and ingredients. What kind of substance do they think will result? Will it be doughy? Hard? Runny? After children make their predictions, have them measure and mix the goop. As they work, invite them to share observations about their mixtures and results. Then provide several plastic containers of different shapes and sizes for children to use as they experiment with and manipulate their alien goop. When finished, have them store the goop in zippered plastic bags to take home and use, with their parents' permission. To extend the experience, send students to the writing center to write about imaginative ways in which they, as aliens, would use the goop in their daily activities.

Alien Goop

1/4 cup cornstarch
1/2 teaspoon Borax
2 tablespoons white glue
1/4 cup warm water
food coloring

Mix the cornstarch and Borax in a disposable plastic bowl. Add the glue and water at the same time. Add a few drops of food coloring. Stir with a craft stick until the ingredients are thoroughly mixed.

Book Links

First Graders from Mars Episode 1: Horus's Horrible Day by Shana Corey (Scholastic, 2001).

Rather than face the new routines and responsibilities of first grade, Horus prefers to cling to sweet memories and the easy life of martiangarten.

Stuart's Cape by Sara Pennypacker (Orchard Books, 2002).

Wearing a cape made from old ties, Stuart embarks on an adventure that helps him put aside his new-school worries—and make a new friend!

When Dinosaurs Go to School by Linda Martin (Chronicle Books, 1999).

Readers discover that a dinosaur's school day is filled with reading, writing, recess, and other fun activities like those that fill a child's school day.

Super Schedules

Name ____________________

Date ____________________

Morning	
Wake up	
Eat breakfast	
Go to school	

Night	
Eat supper	
Take a bath	
Go to bed	

Hello School!
A Classroom Full of Poems

BY DEE LILLEGARD
(ALFRED A. KNOPF, 2001)

In short, inventive verses, common school items take on personalities of their own. A school wakes up early to see who's coming. Paper reveals what its hiding. Glue promises to stick with you through thick and thin. Clock is always on the move. Chair prefers your seat to feet. Beads scatter-chatter, blocks mumble-fumble, and puzzles fall to pieces. Young readers will enjoy looking at school from the fresh perspectives provided in this colorful, eye-appealing book.

Children have probably heard other people's perspectives about school, from parents, siblings, friends and even neighbors. Invite them to share some of the descriptions that others have given them about school—different perspectives on making friends, learning new things, and participating in fun activities. How do these compare to their own experiences at school? After sharing, challenge students to look at school from a different viewpoint—by taking the perspective of things in the school, such as desks, windows, and doors. What, as one of these objects, do they think about school, teachers, and students? How do they describe their role at school? What would they say to people who use them? Conclude by sharing this collection of poems to give children a look at school from the perspective of common school-related objects.

Extending the Book

Who's Coming to School? (Language Arts)

In the poem "School," School wakes up early to see who's coming. At the beginning of each day, use this display to take attendance and to help students get better acquainted. First, make a simple bulletin-board schoolhouse (or purchase one from your local school-supply store). Display the schoolhouse with a large speech

Costume Creations

Use the poem "Costume Box" as a springboard to this creative writing activity. Display a variety of items from your dress-up box, including masks, uniforms, hats, and assorted accessories. Ask children to draw or write a description of a unique costume, choosing only from the articles on display. When finished, have them tell the class about their costume creations. Later, let students put on the actual articles for their costume creations, snap pictures of them, and display the photos or add them to the class album.

bubble labeled "Who's coming to school today?" Then give children sticky notes on which to write their names (these can be reused from day to day). Invite them to take turns answering the school's question by saying "________ is coming to school today," and then placing their sticky notes on the display. After children place their names, encourage them to tell the class an interesting piece of information about themselves.

The Desk in Charge (Math)

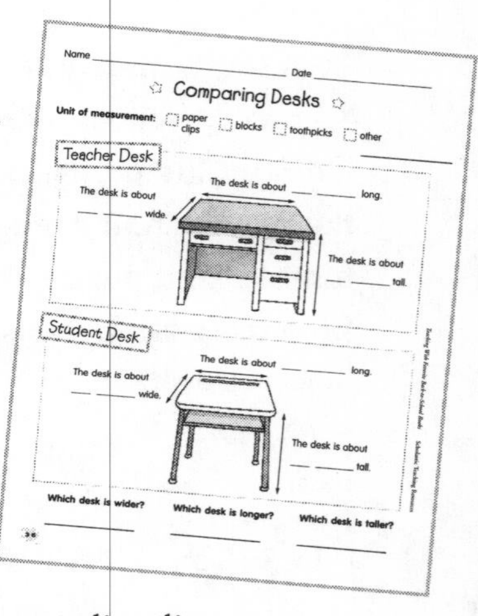

In most classrooms, the teacher's desk *is* impressively large—especially compared to a student desk. Share the poem "Teacher's Desk," then encourage children to find out how the two desks differ in size with this measurement activity. To begin, give them copies of page 36. Have them choose their preferred unit of measurement: paper clips, blocks, toothpicks, or other (have them write the item). After they check their preference, have children measure the width, length, and height of a teacher desk and a student desk. Instruct them to record the answer on each corresponding line, using the appropriate unit of measurement. To measure the height of each desk, they can cut a piece of yarn as tall as the desk and then measure the yarn. When finished, have students share and compare their results.

Paper's Surprise (Language Arts)

Share the poem "Paper," and then invite children to find out what paper is hiding with this fun idea. First, have them use a glue stick to write a simple message or draw a picture on a large sheet of white paper. (So that children can see what they're drawing, have them use colored glue sticks that dry clear.) After the glue dries, pass the papers out at random (making sure children don't get their own pages), and give them chubby pencils. Have children rub the side of the pencil lead lightly over their papers to reveal the hidden message or picture. Invite them to share their paper surprises with the class.

Flocks of Words (Language Arts)

Students' spelling skills will take flight with this simple wordplay activity. First, put a set of magnetic letters in a basket. Place the basket and a magnet board in a center. Then have student pairs visit the center. Encourage the partners to work together to first alphabetize the letters and then "flock" groups of letters together to create words. For inspiration, and to check spelling, have the pair refer to words found around the room, such as on displays, the word wall, book covers, and so on.

Talking School Supplies (Language Arts)

Several poems in the book take the voice of common school supplies—a pencil, paper, crayon, scissors, and glue. Have children make these pencil-box booklets to give voice to common supplies they use in school. First, ask them to cut out copies of the pencil box patterns on page 37. Then give them several quarter-sheets cut from 8 1/2- by 11-inch white paper. Instruct children to draw a type of school supply on each page. Or, have them cut out and glue pictures of school supplies onto the pages. On the back of each page, have students write something that the item on the front might say if it could speak. (More advanced students can enclose the lines of speech in quotation marks.) After completing the pages, help children stack and staple them between the front and back covers, as shown. Invite children to share the contents of their pencil boxes with classmates.

Rhyming Riddles (Language Arts and Logical Reasoning)

Select a number of poems from the book and use them to promote students' reasoning skills. To do this, write each poem on a separate note card, omitting the title. Put the "riddle" cards facedown in a basket. Then invite children to take turns drawing a card, reading the poem, and guessing the subject (title) of the poem. For younger children, you might display objects and pictures to represent the selected poems. Then, if children have difficulty identifying the subject, they can refer to the display for help.

The Bug in Teacher's Coffee and Other School Poems
by Kalli Dakos
(HarperCollins, 1999).

Short, humorous poems reveal the secret thoughts of a pencil, a math test, monkey bars, a bug in a cup of coffee, and many more things found at school.

Lunch Money and Other Poems About School
by Carol Diggory Shields
(Puffin Books, 1995).

Deciding to take or buy lunch, solving math problems, and feeling relieved to have a substitute teacher are only a few of the topics included in this collection of comical verse.

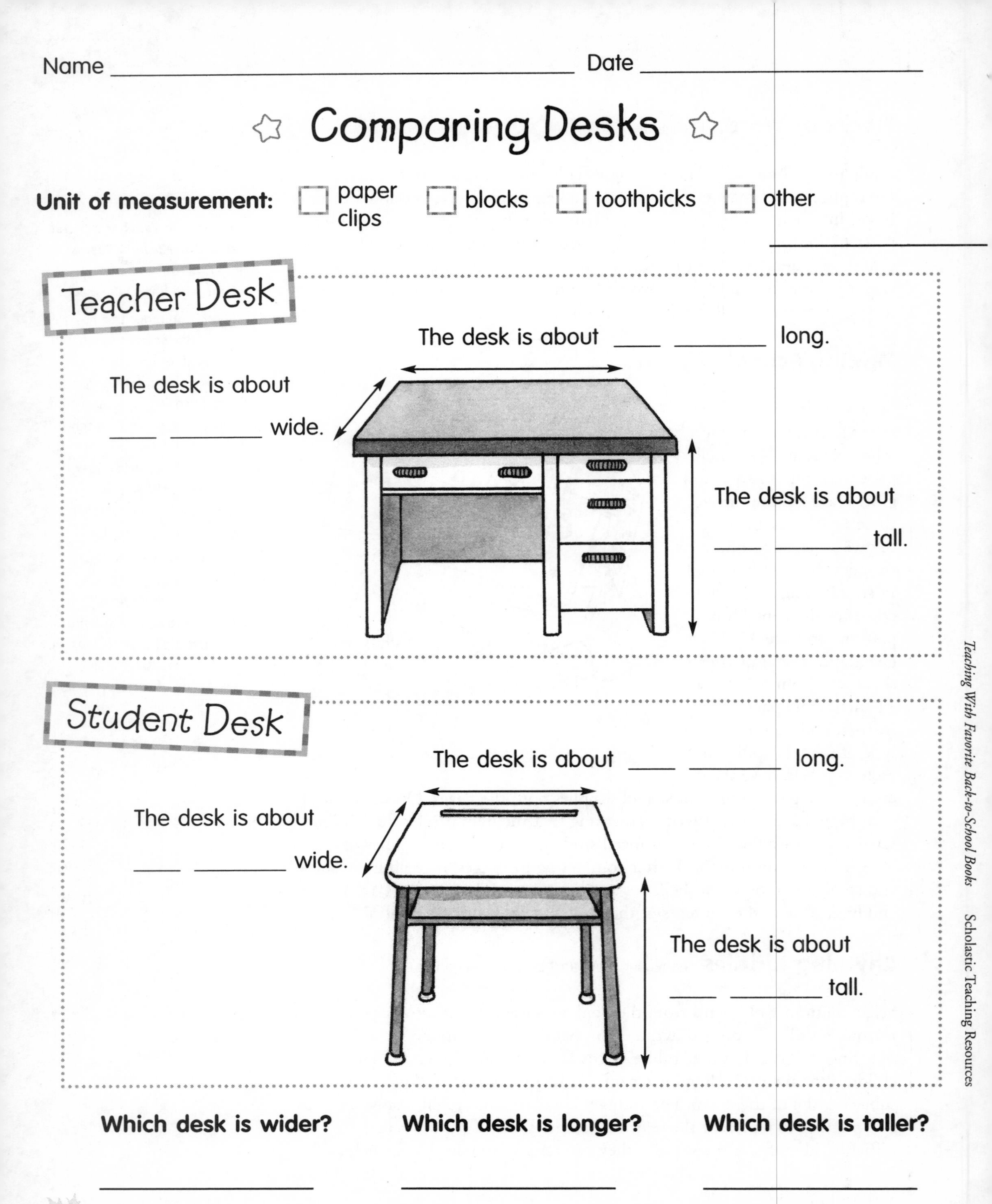
Name
Date
Comparing Desks
Unit of measurement:
paper clips
blocks
toothpicks
other
Teacher Desk
The desk is about ____ ________ long.
The desk is about ____ ________ wide.
The desk is about ____ ________ tall.
Student Desk
The desk is about ____ ________ long.
The desk is about ____ ________ wide.
The desk is about ____ ________ tall.
Which desk is wider?
Which desk is longer?
Which desk is taller?
Teaching With Favorite Back-to-School Books Scholastic Teaching Resources

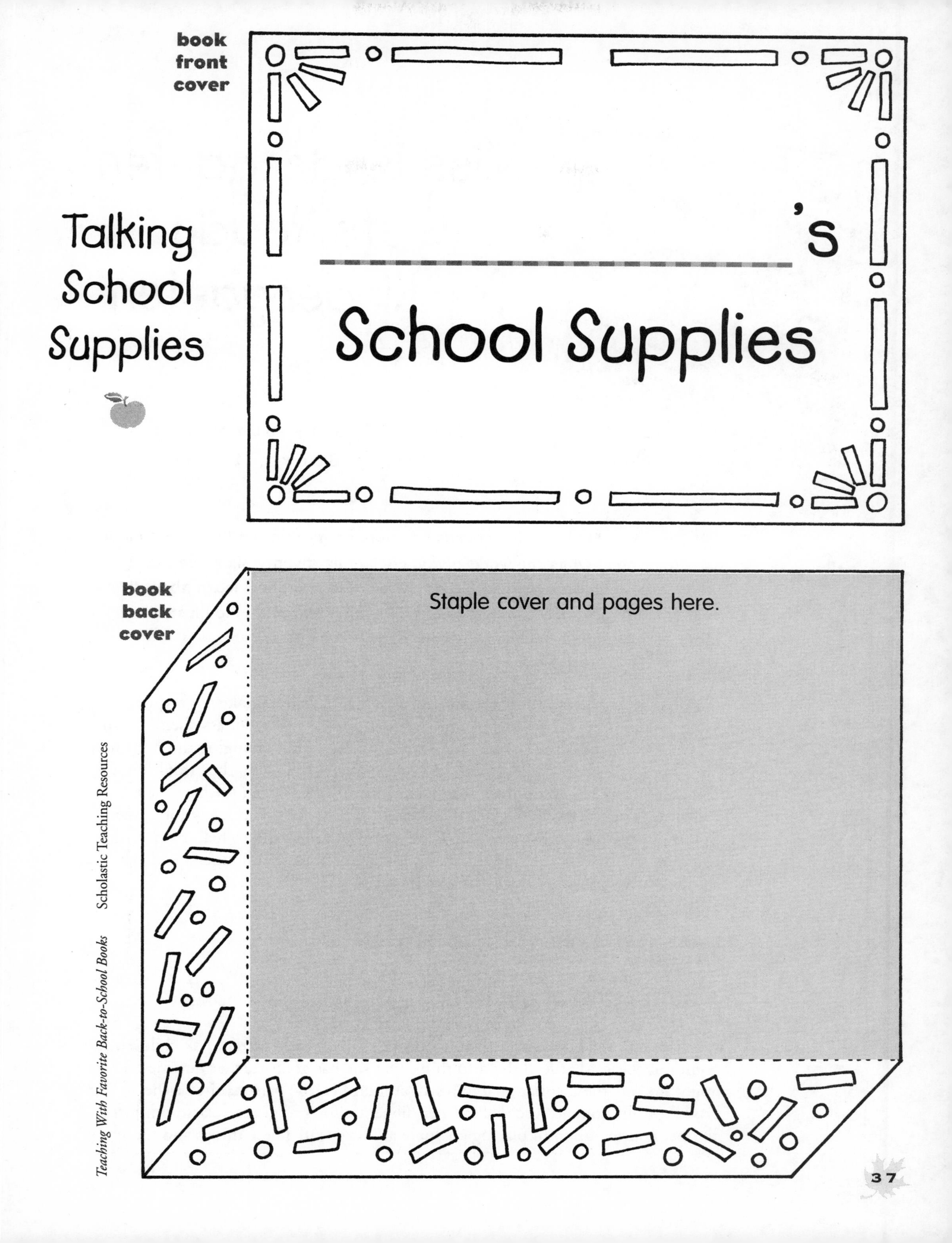
book
front
cover
Talking
School
Supplies
's
School Supplies
book
back
cover
Staple cover and pages here.

Miss Bindergarten Gets Ready for Kindergarten

BY JOSEPH SLATE
(PUFFIN BOOKS, 1996)

Busy Miss Bindergarten spends her morning getting ready for the first day of school. While she works away, each of her twenty-six kindergarten students also prepares for the big day. From A to Z, readers learn about this cast of kindergarten characters through rhyming text and bold illustrations laced with humorous touches on every page.

After gathering students together, have them take a few quiet moments to examine the classroom. As they do, ask them to think about the process of decorating the room, arranging the furniture, shelving books, and placing materials. How do they think these things got done? Who do they imagine did them? Invite them to share their thoughts. Then describe the actual process of getting the room ready for school. Tell about the things that you did, as well as what others did to help prepare the room for the first day of school. Finally, ask children to tell about some of the things that they did personally to prepare for school.

Extending the Book

A Quilt of Great Qualities (Language Arts and Social Studies)

Page through the book with students to study Miss Bindergarten. Ask children to point out things that lead them to think that she has good-teacher qualities. These might include the inspirational notes all around her, the personal items she brought from home to use in class, her diligent efforts to get the classroom just-so, and her consideration in placing an apple at every seat. These things and more suggest that Miss Bindergarten is a caring, conscientious teacher who intends to do her best to teach important skills to her students. Work with children to create a list of qualities they believe make a good teacher (such as "laughs and smiles," "teaches math," "helps us with our work," "reads lots of books," and so on). Then give them 9-inch paper squares to decorate with symbols or pictures to show a good-teacher quality. Assemble the completed squares into a quilt. Display the quilt near your desk to serve as a personal reminder of the teacher qualities that are meaningful and important to your students.

smiles
writes funny stories
nice
lets us use computers
teaches ABCs
ABC
teaches math
4+4=8
gives us sweets
BINGO
helps
plays ball
listens
reads
plays games

Zany Class Zoo (Language Arts)

In the story, each student's name starts with the same letter that begins the name of the animal it represents. Brainstorm and list names of animals that begin with the first letters of your students' names. Then ask children to pick an animal from the list that begins with the same letter as their first name. Have them draw themselves as that animal at school. Or, invite them to use craft items to create 3-D models of their animal selves. When finished, have students write a few interesting, imaginative things about themselves as animals at school. Display each child's animal project and paper together.

Word Family Fun (Language Arts)

To create rhyming text, the author used students' last names that ended with spellings identical to particular words in the story (*Hess* and *dress*, *Lister* and *sister*, and so on). Explain to children that words that have the same word ending belong to the same word family. Ask children to search the pages of the book to find common words and picture names, such as *day*, *dress*, *bunny*, *bike*, *bag*, *book*, *rug*, *pan*, *block*, and *car*. Write these on chart paper. Then work with students to create word family lists for as many of the words as possible. Afterward, invite children to use the lists to write and illustrate word family sentences (for instance, "We found a bug in the mug on the rug.").

Storybook Teacher Favorites

Ask children to name their favorite storybook teachers. Some might include Mr. Slinger from *Lilly's Purple Plastic Purse*, Mrs. Sarah Jane Hartwell from *First Day Jitters*, Miss Nelson from *Miss Nelson Is Missing*, or Ms. Frizzle from *The Magic School Bus* series. Encourage students to explain why a particular storybook teacher appeals to them. Then have them write about and illustrate their favorites. Display their work in the reading center with the title "Our Favorite Storybook Teachers."

A Bird's Eye View

Miss Bindergarten's bird was with her for every step of her kindergarten preparations. Examine with students the pictures of the bird to discover how it was helpful, but also a bit silly and mischievous. Then ask children to write journal entries from the bird's perspective. Have them include things that the bird did, how it helped, how it felt about getting ready for kindergarten, and what it thought of the children and class activities. When finished, invite them to add illustrations to their writing.

Star Students (Science and Language Arts)

Point out Miss Bindergarten's apple necklace to students. Tell them that a special surprise is hidden in every apple. Then cut an apple crosswise to reveal the star-shaped pattern of seeds inside. Explain to children that the star in the apple represents the qualities growing inside each one of them—qualities that make them star students. Discuss some of these behaviors or traits: works hard, listens well, follows directions, does his or her best, completes work, respects school materials, and treats classmates well. Then invite children to follow the directions below to make apple necklaces that highlight their personal star-student qualities.

1. Color and cut out the apple pattern on page 42. (Set aside the seed patterns for now.) Then trace the apple onto a sheet of 8 1/2- by 11-inch white paper, and cut it out.

2. Cut along the dotted lines on the colored apple.

3. Glue the colored apple to the white apple cutout, gluing only around the edges. Trap a loop of green yarn in the glue at the top of the apple.

4. Cut out the five seed patterns. Write a star-student quality that personally applies to you on each seed. Color the seeds light brown.

5. Fold back each flap on the apple. Glue a seed to the apple backing under each flap, forming a star shape, as shown.

6. To make a necklace, thread the apple onto a length of green yarn. Cut and thread short pieces of colored straws onto the yarn on both sides of the apple. Tie the ends of the necklace together.

7. Put on the necklace. Then lift each apple flap to reveal a seed labeled with one of your star-student qualities.

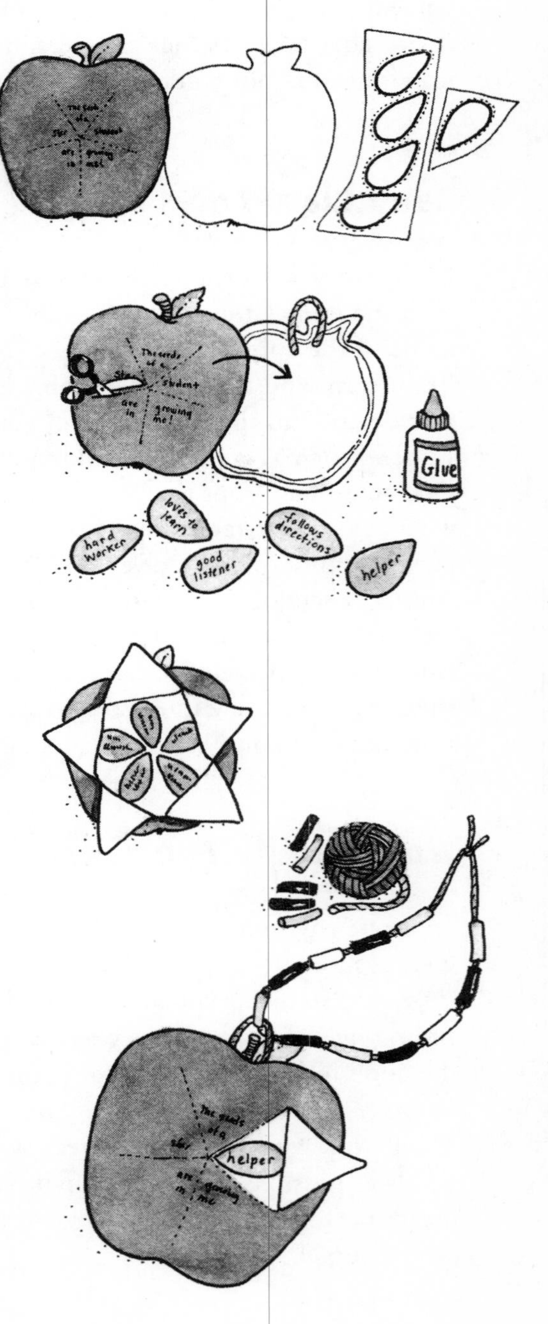

Story Detectives (Language Arts and Reasoning Skills)

Equip students with spyglass props and several copies of the book. Then invite them to become story detectives to answer the following questions. As they work, encourage children to use alphabet, context, and picture clues from the story. Each time children answer a question correctly, have them explain how they arrived at the answer. Add your own questions to further challenge students' reasoning and alphabet sequencing skills.

- What did Miss Bindergarten do before 7:00? (*wake up, wash her face, get dressed, eat breakfast, read the newspaper, pack her car, and drive to school*)
- What was the first thing Miss Bindergarten set up in her classroom? (*the bookshelf*)
- What did Fran do before she left for school? (*She kissed her sister.*)
- Which student boarded the bus before Noah? (*Matty*) After Noah? (*Ophelia*)
- Were Ursula and Vicky on the bus? How do you know? (*No. They were on the sidewalk ahead of Sara, who was first to get off the bus.*)
- In what season does the story take place? (*fall or autumn*)
- Who reached the school first, Lenny or Tommy? Explain your answer. (*Tommy. He was on the school sidewalk before Lenny got across the street.*)
- What was the last thing Miss Bindergarten did to prepare her room? (*She put an apple at every child's seat.*)
- What time did students arrive in class? (*9:00*)
- What did Zach do after he entered the room? (*He found his chair.*)

Getting Ready for School (Language Arts)

Encourage children to make these booklets to examine their routines for kicking off the school day. First, have them stack two 8 1/2- by 11-inch sheets of white paper together, with the top page about one inch above the bottom page. Ask them to fold and staple the pages together to create a layered booklet, as shown. Then, starting with the top page and ending with the bottom page, have them write one of the following along the lower edge of each page: "Getting Up," "Getting out the Door," "Getting to School," and "Getting the School Day Started." Finally, invite children to complete each page by writing about and drawing activities they do during that part of each school day. For example, for "Getting Up," children might draw themselves getting dressed by the bed, or washing their face and brushing their teeth. When finished, encourage children to share their booklets with classmates and, later, with family members.

Book Links

The Awful Aardvarks Go to School by Reeve Lindbergh (Viking, 1997).

From A to Z, the Aardvarks find a variety of ways to make school absolutely awful for their new classmates.

Lilly's Purple Plastic Purse by Kevin Henkes (Greenwillow, 1996).

Lilly loves school! And she loves Mr. Slinger—even after he put away her special purse and glasses for the day. An endearing tale of understanding and mutual respect between student and teacher.

My Teacher's My Friend by P. K. Hallinan (Ideal Children's Books, 1989).

Rhyming text and colorful illustrations feature a teacher and her class engaged in a variety of fun activities.

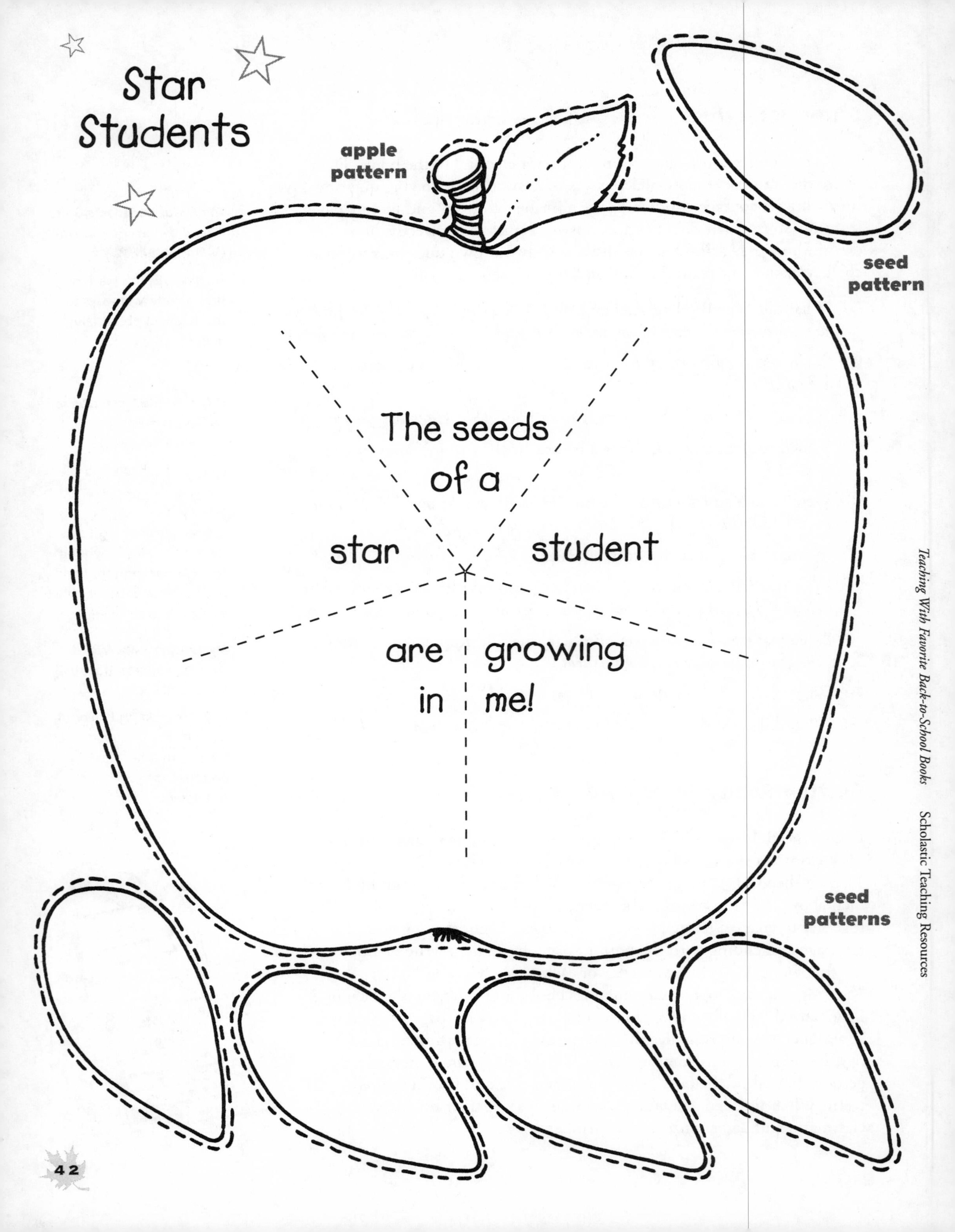
Star Students
apple pattern
seed pattern
The seeds of a star student are growing in me!
seed patterns

Wemberly Worried

BY KEVIN HENKES (GREENWILLOW BOOKS, 2000)

Wemberly is a worrier. She worries about big things, small things, and in-between things. So it's no surprise that the first day of school turns into her biggest worry ever. In spite of her parents' constant reassurances, Wemberly carries her worries to school on the first day. Then she meets Jewel and Nibblet, fellow worriers. Before long, her busy day is over—and so are most of her worries!

Worry Pockets (Language Arts)

Invite students to make these special bunny pockets to communicate to you their first-day and first-week school worries. Post each child's bunny in his or her personal space. Then, as a worry arises, encourage the child to write it on a note card, insert the card into the worry pocket, and raise the bunny's ear. Answer each child's worry with a personal note tucked into the worry pocket. Then lower the bunny's ear to indicate that you have responded. Also make time to privately discuss the child's worry with him or her.

- Color and cut out the bunny patterns on page 44.
- Seal a letter-size envelope, cut it in half, and glue one of the halves onto the bunny to make a pocket. (The open edge should face up.)
- Glue the arms to the bunny pocket.
- Attach the ear with a paper fastener.

Wave Away the Worries (Social Studies)

Tell students that, like Wemberly, we all worry at one time or another. But often, we can wave our worries away soon after they arrive. With this activity, children can share first-day worries that they have already waved good-bye to. To begin, children trace their hands and cut out the outlines. On one side of the cutout they write a first-day worry that has been resolved. Then they write about or illustrate its solution on the other side. Finally, children glue a craft stick to their cutouts. Invite children to share their puppets with the class, waving them in the air as they tell about how they solved, or waved good-bye to, their worries.

Countdown to Kindergarten by Alison McGhee (Silver Whistle, 2002).

An almost-kindergartner counts down to the first day of school—the day she *must* know how to tie her shoes. But when she doesn't learn in time, this worried kindergartner is in for a pleasant surprise.

Jessica by Kevin Henkes (Greenwillow, 1989).

Ruthie projects her first-day worries onto her imaginary friend, Jessica. Then she discovers a real Jessica right in her own classroom!

Oliver Pig at School by Jean Van Leeuwen (Dial Books, 1990).

On the way to school, Oliver is overcome with first-day worries. Once he settles into his classroom, though, Oliver forgets his fears and even makes a friend out of the class troublemaker.

Worry Pockets

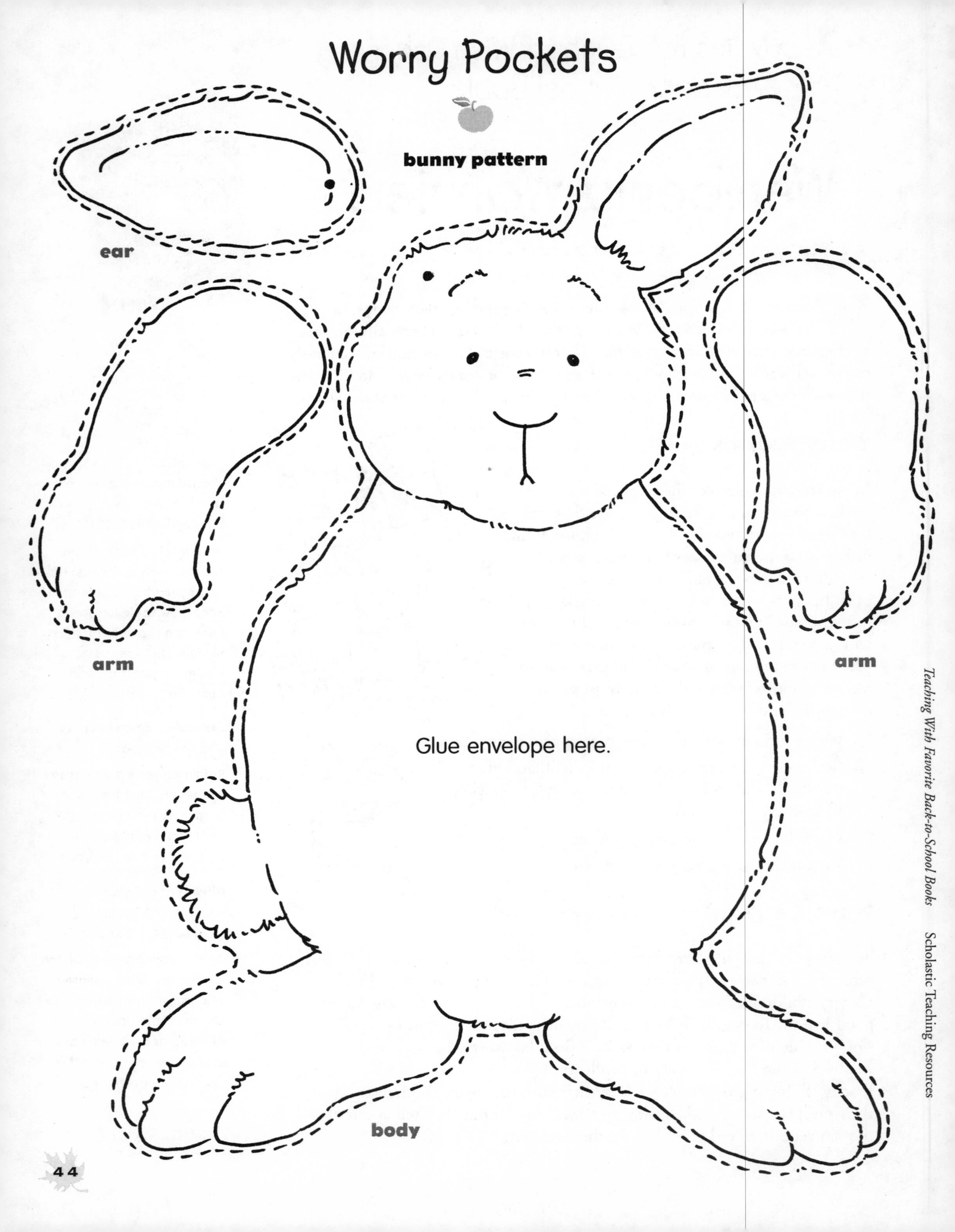

The Kissing Hand

BY AUDREY PENN (CHILD & FAMILY PRESS, 1993)

After planting a gentle kiss in the palm of Chester's hand and tenderly wrapping his fingers around the warm, tingly sensation, Mrs. Raccoon explains that he now has a Kissing Hand—a reminder that her love stays with him wherever he goes. That night, Chester happily dances off to school, but not without leaving Mrs. Raccoon a reminder of his love for her—a special Kissing Hand from him.

Raccoon Reassurances (Language Arts and Art)

Have children imagine they are older raccoons at Chester's school. Ask them to write letters of encouragement to the young critter. Instruct them to include sights, sounds, and activities that Chester can expect to see, hear, and do in his new class, especially the fun and interesting things that a young raccoon might enjoy. Then invite children to create paper-plate raccoon masks to wear while they read their letters aloud.

"Hand-y" Love Magnet (Art)

Students may wonder if grownups experience separation anxiety when they leave their kids at school. Explain that, often, adults are just as nervous about leaving their little ones as the little ones are about being left to experience new things. Then invite children to make these magnetic ornaments to leave with parents or caregivers as handy reminders that their love stays with the adult even when they are at school.

1. Give each child one hand pattern from page 46 to cut out. Then direct students to cut out the center opening and back it with their photo, or a picture they've drawn of themselves.

2. Have them write their name on the line. Laminate the cutout.

3. Tell children to add a bow to the front of the cutout and a piece of magnetic tape to the back.

Billy and the Big New School by Catherine & Laurence Anholt (Albert Whitman & Company, 1997).

Billy nurses a baby bird to health and sends it off to care for itself. In the process, he realizes that he too must leave the "nest" to begin his first day of school.

Oh My Baby, Little One by Kathi Appelt (Harcourt, 2000).

Mama Bird reassures Baby Bird that the love they share remains with both of them through every moment and movement of the day.

Tom Goes to Kindergarten by Margaret Wild (Albert Whitman & Company, 1999).

When Tom's excitement over school turns to fear, his family stays to help ease him into the new situation. The plan works so well that, the next day, Tom's not the only one who's eager to return to kindergarten!

"Hand-y" Love Magnet

hand patterns

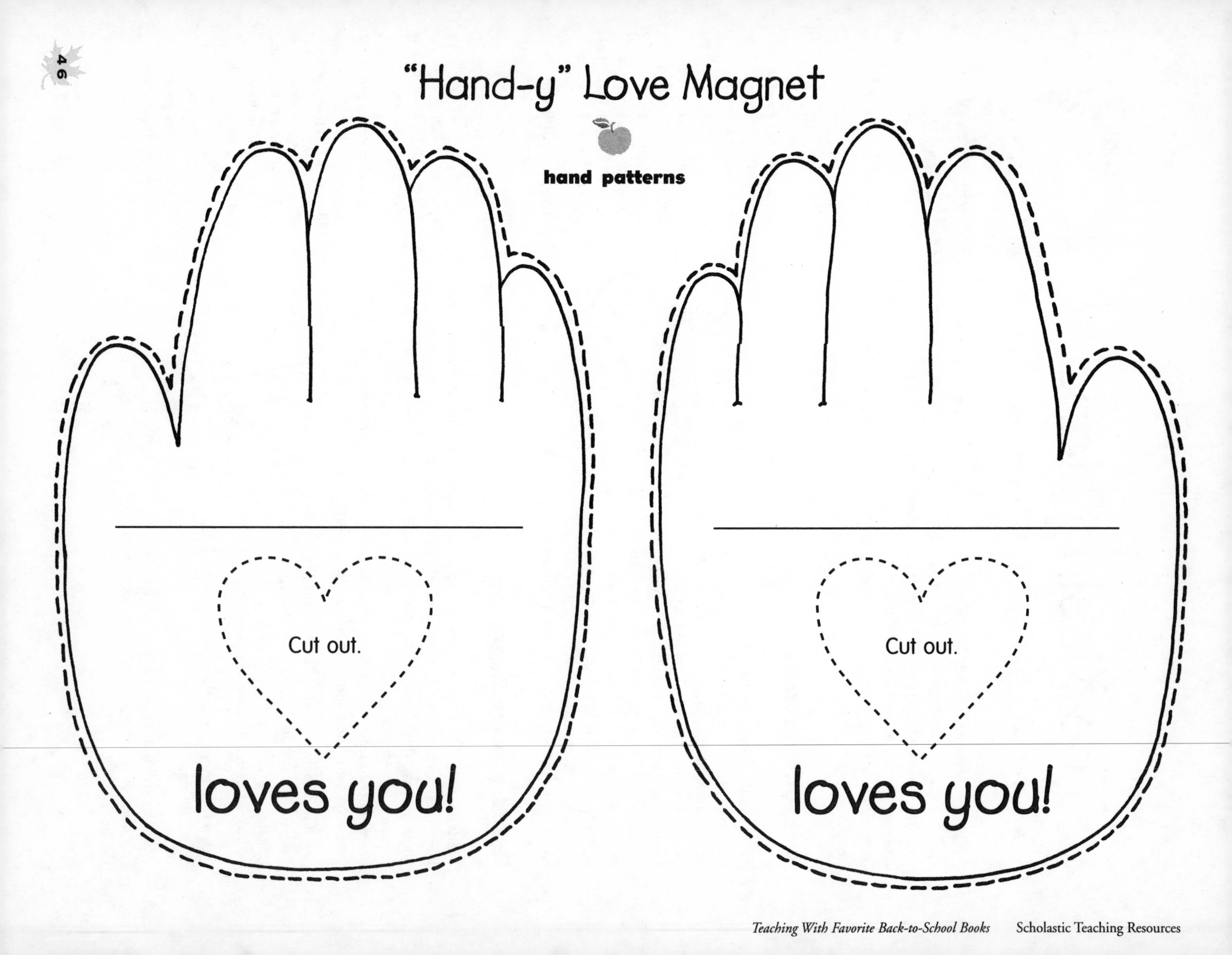

Fabulous First-Week Festivities

Commemorate the first days of school with these fun activities that help children summarize, share, and celebrate their new-school-year experiences. To give children time to settle into and "taste" the many assorted first-of-the-year school experiences, plan to hold your celebration after the first full week of school.

Getting Ready

Enlist the help of students and parents to carry out some of the following preparations for your class celebration.

- Make and send colorful invitations to parents and guests.
- Convert a local newspaper into class news for children and guests to enjoy during the celebration. Give the newspaper a name related to your class. Create an appropriate banner and glue it over the original one. Then glue child- and teacher-composed stories, photos, and student illustrations about first-day experiences onto the pages of the newspaper.
- Prepare the fruit for "Fruity New Year Pie" (see "Enjoy a Snack," page 48) and bring in additional snack foods and drinks.
- Assemble individual party bags that contain symbolic items. You might include star stickers (for the star student inside each child), glue sticks (for friends to stick with during the year), erasers (to erase mistakes and bad habits), pencils and small notepads (for recording great school memories), and a small bag of trail mix (for the learning trail to be blazed in the new year). Pass out the party bags at the end of the celebration.
- Decorate the classroom with festive streamers, balloons, a "Happy New School Year!" banner, and copies of students' favorite back-to-school books.
- Write short, inspirational messages on festive sticky notes. Stick a note in each child's personal space on the day of the celebration.

Celebrate!

Sign In

Station a blank book and colored markers on a table at the door. Invite students and guests alike to each sign a page in the book. Encourage them to personalize the page with art, notes, and quotes that represent their new-school-year excitement and good wishes for a great year of fun and learning.

Make Personal Party Hats

Invite children to represent themselves by decorating 9-inch paper plates with colors, designs, and pictures. Help them cut a line to the center of the plate, shape the plate into a cone party hat, and staple the ends in place. If desired, let children add curly ribbons to the top of their hats. Then have them add yarn ties. Encourage children to wear their party hats during the first-week festivities.

Play a Get-Acquainted Game

Play this guessing game to help children become better acquainted. First, ask children to write a few things about themselves on large note cards, but not to sign their names. Put the cards in an empty book bag. Then invite children to take turns removing a card from the bag, reading it silently, and circulating around the room to try to identify the described child. When a player thinks he or she has identified the mystery person, have him or her tap that child on the head. Ask the selected child to confirm or deny the player's guess. If wrong, the player guesses again. If correct, the identified child becomes the next player.

Hold a Schedule Relay

Have children review their class schedule with this "Schedule Skedaddle" relay. To prepare, label pairs of note cards with each activity shown on your class schedule. Then gather pairs of items to represent each activity. For instance, use books for reading, plastic numbers for math, magnifying glasses for science, rhythm sticks for music, lunchboxes for lunch, and paintbrushes for art. Spread the cards out on one end of a table and the items on the other end. Display the class schedule nearby. Divide the class into teams and station the teams across the room from the table. Explain that, on a signal, the first player on each team walks quickly to the table to find a card labeled with the first activity on the schedule. Then the player finds the corresponding item at the other end of the table. The player takes the item back to his or her team and tags the next player. Play continues in this manner until a team has collected and correctly sequenced its cards and items for the entire class schedule.

Enjoy a Snack

To celebrate the fruitful year that lies ahead, invite each child to create a nutritious Fruity New Year Pie. Set out an individual-size graham cracker pie crust for each child. Add containers of different fruits, such as watermelon cubes, grape halves, sliced strawberries, blueberries, cantaloupe cubes, apple chunks, and orange wedges. Also include a container of vanilla yogurt. Have children fill their pie shells with the fruits of their choice and then top their pies with a dollop of yogurt. Invite them to enjoy their fruity treats with a cool serving of apple juice. (Check for food allergies before serving snacks to children.)

Make a Time Capsule

Give children work and art samples created during their first days of school. Ask them to choose one or two personal pieces from the samples to add to a class time capsule. Put students' selections in a plastic sweater box, along with copies of the class roster and schedule, photos of children from the first school days, summaries of books shared the first week of class (and copies of the books, if available), the class newspaper from your first-week festivities, instant photos taken during the celebration, and any other significant items related to the first days of school. Tell children that, at the end of the school year, they will open the time capsule and review the items to compare the changes in themselves, the class, the room, and their schedule that have occurred since the beginning of the year. Then, with great ceremony and fanfare, "seal" the time capsule and store it away to conclude your first-week festivities.